Distance Learning for Higher Education

AN ANNOTATED BIBLIOGRAPHY

Marjorie Fusco
and
Susan E. Ketcham

2002
Libraries Unlimited
A Division of Greenwood Publishing Group, Inc.
Greenwood Village, Colorado

For family and friends with love.
—M.F.

For Daryl and Kaitlin with love.
—S.E.K.

LIBRARIES UNLIMITED
7730 East Belleview Avenue, Suite A200
Greenwood Village, CO 80111
1-800-255-5800
www.lu.com

Library of Congress Cataloging-in-Publication Data

Fusco, Marjorie, 1941-
    Distance learning for higher education : an annotated
bibliography / Marjorie Fusco and Susan E. Ketcham.
        p. cm.
    Includes bibliographical references and index.
    ISBN 1-56308-847-9 (pbk.)
    1. Distance education--Bibliography. 2. University
extension--Bibliography. I. Ketcham, Susan E., 1956- II. Title.
Z5814.D54 F78 2002

[LC5800]
016.3713'5--dc21   2002003184

Contents

Acknowledgments

We wish to sincerely thank Carlos Pinder Jr. (Dowling College) and Elizabeth Herbert (Southampton College of Long Island University) for all their time and efforts in pursuing materials for us through interlibrary loan. Thanks also to our colleagues Mary Brazezicke, Virginia Ehlers, Elizabeth Gentilella, and Donna Headley (Dowling College) and Robert Gerbereux and William Roberson (Southampton College of Long Island University) for their continued support.

Introduction

During the last several years there has been a proliferation in the literature on distance education and the advances in technology that drive its growth. All of education, from elementary and higher education to education in the workplace and lifelong learning, has experienced the growing number of options for distance learning and delivery systems. International Data Corporation (IDC), a market research firm, stated there was an estimated 55 percent increase in the number of institutions of higher education taking the online plunge in 2001.[1] IDC also predicted that by 2004 more than 3,300 online courses (up from 1,500 in 1999) will be available in the United States. This growth is expected to be especially strong in academic and corporate education. According to the IDC, the U.S. education department estimates there are more than 230,000 providers targeting some 138 million students or clients in school and corporate communities.[2] Projections are that the academic market in the United States will rise from about $334 million in 2000 to an estimated $744 million in 2004. The cost of staff, hardware, communication services, and related support for distant learning will bring the total to almost $3 billion by then.[3] This phenomenon is transforming the virtual learning environment, where education can take place anywhere and at any time. Presently colleges and universities offer anywhere from a few distance learning courses to entire degree programs. Corporations use the same methods for employee education and training. For-profit educational organizations have also entered the educational arena, bringing with them a whole new set of concerns for both academia and potential learners.

This book provides a survey of the literature on many current distance learning concerns, such as competition from nontraditional education, costs for running distance learning programs, planning issues, selection of appropriate distance learning modalities, training and compensation for faculty, curriculum and instructional design, pedagogy, course and program evaluation, student education and assessment, and the formation of collaborative partnerships between institutions or between institutions and businesses. The selections we discuss constitute recommended reading for administrators of academic institutions as they struggle to survive economically in fast-changing competitive educational markets, which are more than qualified to provide good education and which must meet the needs of this next generation of learners. Individuals in the business sector will also find these selections a helpful resource. Forming a distance education partnership with a college or university can enable them to provide continuing education and training for their workforce. This information can also be a valuable resource for anyone who wants to learn more about distance learning—its role in today's educational environment and in society.

The material we cover comes from professional journals, individual papers taken from the proceedings of recent distant learning conferences, documents from professional organizations or institutions on the Web, books and chapters from books that review specific topics, and studies related to distance learning. A selective body of research is reviewed from the most current literature (1999 to the present) due to the rapid changes occurring in distance education. However, some of the literature may include earlier studies if they reinforce pedagogy of interest to educators or if we deem the information relevant to the needs of campus administrative leaders or public policy makers.

The annotated bibliography is organized thematically. It is not meant to describe in depth the experiences or practices of any one institution; rather, we hope that the annotations provide information helpful to the reader. We encourage readers to obtain the whole article, paper, document, or book for a complete analysis of the study or information they need. Materials can be found in most academic institutions that subscribe to these sources or obtained through interlibrary loan from one's own library (public or private).

Chapter 1 offers several definitions of virtual or distance learning. Chapter 2 reviews the literature on the various methods of distance learning delivery options, including the Web-based technology of broadcast education models used by colleges and universities. Chapter 3 reviews the literature on administrative issues for higher education—from the planning process to program evaluation. Chapter 4 focuses on the learning community itself, including issues of interest to faculty and students as they teach and learn in the virtual environment. Chapter 5 reviews distance learning programs and curriculum development. Of equal importance is the discussion of the role of the library and other support services found in Chapter 6. Chapter 7 provides a listing of higher education resources such as accrediting bodies. The role of these bodies is to ensure adherence to standards of quality for education. They will continue to guide academic institutions as the virtual learning environment evolves and transforms the nature of higher education. This chapter also lists other associations and organizations involved in higher education. Most education associations or organizations can now be found on the Web. They are valuable resources that present the latest information on trends and issues in distance learning. Listservs and discussion groups act as a forum for discussing issues and new developments in the field. Other resources include journals dedicated to the topic of distance learning, media such as videotapes, and Websites devoted to distance learning information. Finally, Chapter 8 lists additional paper resources that will be valuable to those involved in developing and ensuring quality in distance learning programs.

Throughout the bibliographic annotations and the list of Websites, Web addresses (URLs) are included. Due to the continually evolving nature of the Web, these addresses may change over time. Professional organizations usually do not change their URLs; however, they may change the URL for a document, remove the document entirely, or replace it with newer information. We therefore recommend that the reader check these sites occasionally for new developments or information. New sites for distance learning appear every day on the Web, and new organizations may develop as well. Good reliable sites containing information are those that have .edu (educational site) or .org (professional association or organization) included in their URL. The reader may also explore the Web for information by using a search engine such as the ones at http://www.yahoo.com, http://www.excite.com, or http://www.altavista.com. The search engine itself provides specific examples of how to type in a search term.

NOTES

1.   Chris Johnston, "Net Study Fever Hits America." *The Times Higher Education Supplement.* No. 1477 (2001): 14. (9 pars.). Online. Lexis Nexis. (13 March 2002).

2.   Ibid.

3.   Ibid.

Virtual Learning

DISTANCE LEARNING DEFINED

The purpose of this chapter is to examine the nature of virtual learning, to identify the parties involved in this environment, and to review definitions of the terminology often used in the literature. Bauman (2000) looks at online learning communities and their students. To preserve the nature of student learning in the evolving virtual learning environment, he proposes a set of guidelines for them to follow both in and outside of class. Hanson et al. (1997) provide a number of definitions of distance education. Wolf and Johnstone (1999) set out to establish a consistent language for the different terms that people often use to describe the virtual learning environment. They have designed both a taxonomy of the various institutional settings in which virtual learning can take place and a framework that describes how course and content development, mentoring, and assessment tasks are matched to particular types of technology. The Washington State Higher Education Coordinating Board's definition is another attempt to describe the teachers and students, instruction, content, and assessment techniques used in distance learning. We hope that these articles will set the stage for a better understanding of the nature of distance education in an expanding virtual environment.

◀ Bauman, Marcy. **Online Learning Communities.** URL: http://leahi.kcc
.hawaii.edu/org/tcc_conf97/pres/bauman.html (6 August 2001).

Addressing the distant learner's need for social interaction, Bauman views online learning communities as "places where they can test assumptions, try out new ideas, and ask questions of other learners." Bauman says that "students need skills, to be sure, but they also need the predispositions and habits of mind that will enable them to be creative, flexible learners throughout their lifetimes, not just during the years when they are in school." Bauman states that students face certain challenges in creating online communities (e.g., they need to play a much more active role and must have the skills to survive in an online class or program). The difficulties students face are: (1) persistence in writing back and forth with others to get answers to their questions; (2) the ability to analyze a problem and phrase questions that will elicit the answers they seek; and (3) the predisposition to read for information that they then use. Bauman similarly discusses the difficulties confronting instructors (e.g., the lack of verbal and visual clues, experience in online writing assignments, experience in answering questions online, and experience with the level of online contact required). Bauman presents a list of guidelines for creating communities within individual classes, as well as outside of class so that college remains a place for students to encounter ideas and challenges and to develop habits of mind that are the hallmarks of education.

◀ **Distance Learning in Virginia: Trends and Policy Issues for 1998 and Beyond.** URL: http://www.schev.edu/html/reports/dlreport.html (7 August 2001).

In a report they prepared for the State Council of Higher Education for Virginia, New Dominion Partners (9 January 1998) define distance learning as "[a]ny formal approach to learning that takes instruction to the learner rather than taking the learner to instruction." Their report also states that the term is often interchangeable with "virtual learning."

In recognizing the potential of distance learning as well as the changes in the technology, practices, and traditions of higher education, the council wanted to address the broad policy issues surrounding distance learning. The questions the council set out to address were the following: (1) What trends are catalysts for distance learning initiatives? (2) What are the emerging issues surrounding distance learning in Virginia that need attention in the near future?

The council asked a number of people from colleges and universities, state government, and businesses in Virginia and other states for their views. The trends they cited most often were changing consumer demands, expanding markets, economic development needs, key technology developments, virtual universities, and for-profit ventures in higher education—companies entering the higher education arena as partners with or as competitors of traditional nonprofit institutions. A number of coordinating and regulatory issues emerged that included relationships with virtual universities, program duplication, accreditation and program approval, consumer protection, and information resources. Additional issues pertained to faculty development, roles, rewards, and the use of technology.

◀ Hanson, Dan, Nancy J. Maushak, Charles A. Schlooser, Mary L. Anderson, Christine Sorensen, and Michael Simonson. **Distance Education: Review of the Literature**, 2d edition. Washington, D.C.: Association for Educational Communications and Technology and Research Institute for Studies in Education, 1997. ISBN 0892401060.

This book gives a brief, yet comprehensive, overview of the literature on distance education in the United States. It provides a number of definitions of distance education, several distance education theories by leaders in the field, an overview of the history of distance education, a summary of distance education research, and a selected bibliography of distance education literature. The authors define distance education as follows:

> "[D]istance education" is education that takes place in different places at the same time when telecommunications are used. Students can also learn at different times and in different places—the purest form argued by some.[1]

However, distance education also includes many other definitions. For example:

> Distance education takes place when a teacher and student(s) are separated by physical distance and technology (i.e., audio, video, data, and print), often in combination with face-to-face communication, is used to bridge the instructional gap.[2]

> The term distance learning is often interchanged with distance education. However, this is inaccurate since institutions/instructors control educational delivery while the student is responsible for learning. In other words, distance learning is the result of distant education. Another term that has experienced some recent popularity is distributed education. This term may represent the trend to utilize a mix of delivery modes for optimal instruction and learning.[3]

◀ Wolf, David B., and Sally M. Johnstone. **Cleaning up the Language: Establishing a Consistent Vocabulary for Electronically Delivered Academic Programs.** *Change* 31, no. 4 (July/August 1999): 34–39 (32 pars.). Online. Proquest. (25 April 2001).

The authors provide an excellent glossary of terms for administrators. This article describes the current terminology describing distance education, virtual universities, or institutional taxonomies, as well as frameworks for electronic course configurations. People use the terms distance education, distance learning, distributed learning, and virtual university interchangeably to describe a particular type of virtual learning environment. To help clarify the discussions for higher education and rather than developing new labels to describe the numerous content-delivery methods, the authors developed a taxonomy that describes a variety of institutional settings and frameworks that offer electronic coursework. The taxonomy includes, for example, the virtual university (an institution without a campus, such as Western Governors University); the virtual university consortium (accredited academic institutions, such as Colorado Community Colleges On-Line, that do not grant degrees but are linked together online and supply centralized or coordinated coursework to students); an academic services consortium, a virtual program; the virtual certification institution; and the traditional accredited institution with electronic courses.

In their 2000 Master Plan for Higher Education, the Washington State Higher Education Coordinating Board provides yet another definition of distance education:

> Distance learning takes place when teachers and students are separated by physical distance for most of the instructional delivery. The term "distance learning" course or program should only be used if:
>
> - Teachers and students are separated for a predominance of the instructional contact hours.
>
> - The content has been specifically designed as a course of study to increase and assess student knowledge or skills.
>
> - An education institution provides the course content and is responsible for assessment of student achievement through credits, certification, or degrees.[4]

This definition places a responsibility on the institution not only to provide distance learning but also to be accountable for providing quality content to online courses and to be responsible for assessment.

NOTES

1.   M. Simonson. Distance Education Revisited: An Introduction to the Issue. *TechTrends* 40, no. 3 (1995): 2.

2.   Badrul H. Khan, ed. *Web-Based Instruction*. New Jersey: Educational Technology Publications, 1997, 81.

3.   Virginia Steiner. What Is Distance Education? (10 October 1995); available at the following Website: http://www.dlrn.org/library/dl/whatis.html (15 August 2001).

4.   *Distance Learning Enrollments in Independent Institutions: Feasibility Study*. Olympia: State of Washington Higher Education Coordinating Board, 1999, 2.

Methods of Delivery

WEB-BASED INSTRUCTION

Web technology opens up a myriad of teaching initiative possibilities for higher education. In the year 2002, 85 percent of American colleges will be offering online courses to over two million students. Web-based communication will continue to grow rapidly as newer technologies evolve, bandwidth costs fall, and the use of digital satellites, fiber-optic cable, and digital subscriber lines becomes readily available.[1] New technologies combined with Web technology makes possible Web-based instruction, a form of asynchronous communication (i.e., interactions between users that do not take place simultaneously) and an alternative approach to traditional classroom instruction. Web-based courses and resources are appearing on the Web at a rapid rate, bringing with them a revolutionary change in higher education institutions.

Along with the opportunities and benefits of Web-based instruction comes the need to examine its numerous aspects as a means of distance learning. The main considerations for a Web-based course are design, development, delivery, and evaluation. In addition, mutual support and respect need to exist between technical, administrative, and teaching personnel. This also includes the institution's responsibility to provide access to its libraries and other resources online.

The following is a brief description of teaching on the Web and a review of the literature (books, articles, reports, and Web documents) on Web-based instruction.

Asynchronous Communication

Two categories of delivery systems for distance education are synchronous and asynchronous communication. "Synchronous instruction requires the simultaneous participation of all students and instructors. The advantage is that the interaction is done in 'real time.' "[2] Forms of synchronous delivery include interactive TV and audiographics (the combined use of voice transmission, computer networking, and graphics transmission through narrowband telecommunication channels such as facsimile machine, still video system, computers, or electronic drawing systems, e.g., electronic blackboard).[3] Additional forms include computer conferencing (the use of electronic channels to facilitate communication among groups of people at two or more locations via computer), which involves Interactive Relay Chat (IRC)—software that allows real-time electronic conversations among hundreds of users, multi-user domain (MUD), multi-user object oriented (MOO), and videoconferencing systems such as CU-SeeMe (an Internet-based videophone platform used for inexpensive multipoint computer conferencing).[4]

Web-based courses belong to the category of asynchronous communication, in which parties participate at different times. Asynchronous communication offers a choice of where and, above all, when you may access learning. A student can learn at any time and in any place. Web-based instruction is limited to learners with access to the Web and may include hypertext and hypermedia materials. Many learners or a single learner may access instruction at once. Web-based instruction may also include e-mail and links to videotaped courses, correspondence courses, audiocassettes, or listservs. Asynchronous learning can be either an individual or a group learning experience. Interactions with one's instructor and fellow students do not take place simultaneously. Rather, students work at their own pace and contribute to a group discussion by posting comments via the computer or by leaving voice-mail messages. Some online courses may offer a synchronous learning experience through the use of scheduled chat rooms in which students and the professor are online at the same time.

Virtual Classrooms

The virtual classroom exists in the virtual environment known as the Internet. Very much like a "real" class, the virtual class provides the tools learners need; creates an expectation for an environment conducive to learning; brings together educators and learners to share information and exchange ideas; allows learners the freedom to experiment, test their knowledge, practice completing tasks, and apply what they've discussed or read about; provides mechanisms for evaluating performance; and (6) provides a safe haven in which learning can take place.[5] Virtual class learning is also referred to as telelearning or distributed online education. The virtual class is an electronic meeting place of students and lecturers for the purposes of teaching and learning. It is an educational experience involving real people in a virtual dimension. The virtual class takes many forms, for example, online education using the Internet or an intranet, meeting in virtual reality as telepresences, or a combination of these methods.[6]

One example of a virtual classroom is the distance learning efforts of Duke University. Duke's first goal for offering a distance learning program was to reach out to the global market and to attract a diverse group of students. It has now established a global network of students, thus its virtual classroom fosters crucial communication and remote management skills that would otherwise be difficult to learn. Faculty members now interact with people internationally. John Gallagher, a director of computer-mediated learning at Duke, states, "We actually believe that this is going to be the paradigm for education beginning now and into the future."[7]

Statistics in the December 1999 report by the National Center for Education Statistics (NCES) of the U.S. Department of Education (USDE) indicate that in 1997 and 1998, almost 44 percent of all higher education institutions offered distance courses. Larger institutions are moving more rapidly than smaller ones: Of those with more than 10,000 students, 87 percent offered distance classes, whereas only 19 percent of institutions with fewer than 3,000 students did so. Total enrollment in postsecondary, credit-granting distance learning courses in 1997 and 1998 was 1,363,670, and that number has grown considerably since then.[8] According to the U.S. Department of Education, about 84 percent of four-year colleges will offer online distance learning courses by 2002, up from 62 percent in 1998, and the International Data Corporation (IDC), a Massachusetts research firm, reports that community colleges will soar to 90 percent, up from 58 percent.[9]

Distributed Online Education

"There are two facts that universities are trying to deal with today. They are: (1) that universities are trying to rethink their missions and methods for the 21st century; and (2) that new institutions are emerging with different corporate structures with focused missions, and some of them use the methods of distributed learning."[10] There are four models for universities dedicated to distributed learning today: (1) the wholly owned university subsidiary of a for-profit company—for example, the Motorola University and the British Aerospace Virtual University; (2) the for-profit university, of which the University of Phoenix is a prominent example; (3) the for-profit subsidiary of a nonprofit university, of which there are now various examples; and (4) the nonprofit university associated with another nonprofit university outside the United States (e.g., the United States Open University, which uses only distributed learning as a mode of education).[11]

World Wide Web

Who is learning on the Web? Students and faculty from colleges or universities are not the only people studying and learning on the Web. Today businesses, corporations, hospitals—doctors, nurses, pilots, military personnel, and employees from every sector of the workforce—are participating in Web-based programs or courses. The Web enables learners to choose where and when they wish to learn. It has also brought about a shift in the way teaching and learning take place. Learning is becoming much less teacher-centered and much more learner-centered.[12]

Web-based instruction involves more of one's senses and limits instantaneous interaction between learners and educators. It may also require security measures to limit access to learners. Distance learning Web-based courses vary depending on the technology used. For example, a class may be delivered through an audioconference (students can only hear each other), or it may use a two-way video (students can also see each other). Here off-site students are able to participate in the class as it is taking place—in real time. The distance learning instructor develops the Web-based course and usually posts lesson materials and assignments for the course on the Internet. Students read or view these materials at their own convenience. Once they complete the assigned activities, the students send them via computer, fax, or regular mail to the instructor for evaluation. Courses taught through distance learning still must include some form of evaluation of the students. Depending on the type of course and the distance of the student, instructors administer tests through various means. They may require students to come to a campus for the exam or take the exam either at an off-site location or through a two-way video class in order to ensure the exam's integrity.

In order to support communication through the Web for teaching and learning, a number of Web-based tools are necessary. Institutions make extensive use of software such as Netscape (Navigator or Communicator) and Microsoft's Internet Explorer. These tools enable users to access the Web environment. HTML, CGI, and Java are Web-type programming formats or languages that are commonly used to create the most effective Web-based sites.

Researchers at CERN, an organization for nuclear research near Geneva, Switzerland, created the hypertext-based, distributed information system used in the Internet environment. This system allows users to create, edit, or browse hypertext documents accessible through various systems of interconnected links. Different systems highlight hyperlinks differently—some put the link in boldface or in color, while others underline the link. The clients and servers using the Internet are easily accessible. Web-based training and computer-based training are delivered via the Internet.

The following selected articles, books, and documents represent initiatives or programs that colleges and universities in the United States and abroad have developed. This section may also include examples from the private sector that use Web-based instruction as a form of distance education.

◀ Carr-Chellman, Alison A., and Philip Duchastel. **The Ideal Online Course.** *British Journal of Educational Technology* 31, no. 3 (July 2000): 229–41. (48 pars.). Online, FirstSearch. WiSonSelect_FT. Article number BED100021069. (11 March 2002).

The authors discuss distributed learning as the new online paradigm shifts from distance education to learning without having distance, where making learning resources and instructional activities takes precedence over providing instruction. Of interest to the reader is the explanation of threaded asynchronous communication (faculty or students post messages on a Website for others to read); synchronous interchanges through audioconferencing, Internet chats, and videoconferencing are all means of keeping students and instructors interacting.

◀ Gilbertson, Denny, and Jamie Poindexter. **Distance Education Classroom Design: Tips for Designing a Conference and Distance Education Classroom at County Extension Facilities.** 1 May 2000. URL: http://www.uwex.edu/disted/rooms/county.htm (26 July 2001).

This document provides excellent information and tips for planning and developing distance learning classrooms using audio- and videoconferencing, satellites and computers, or desktop systems from the University of Wisconsin Extension Instructional Communications Systems. It explains the use of telecommunication wiring, dial-up audioconferencing, the Educational Teleconference Network (ETN), and audiovisual tips for planners and developers.

◀ Harrison, Nigel. **How to Design Self-Directed and Distance Learning: A Guide for Creators of Web-Based Training, Computer-Based Training, and Self-Study Materials.** New York: McGraw-Hill, 1999. ISBN 0070271003.

This helpful guide provides an easy-to-follow, systematic approach to the essential knowledge and performance aids for designing Web-based, self-directed, or distance learning programs. It covers topics ranging from assessing the need for training to evaluating the results. The guide even provides the following worksheets and tests for designers: (1) designing performance problems for students to solve; (2) selecting and designing the right format; (3) setting measurable, attainable objectives; (4) testing and improving the product; (5) putting the program into action; and (6) assessing its success. The elements of a project for either self-directed or distance learning can include text-based distance learning, computer-based training (CBT), Web-based training, books, workshops, multimedia, workbooks, video, audio, and so on.

◀ Hazemi, Reza, Stephen Hailes, and Steve Wilbur, eds. **The Digital University: Reinventing the Academy**. New York: Springer-Verlag, 1998. ISBN 1852330031.

This book examines the impact that Web-based teaching is having on all aspects of university life including research, support, teaching, and management. The book has five sections: (1) reinventing the academy; (2) challenges that universities face; (3) using technology to meet these challenges; (4) using groupware for teaching and learning; and (5) realizing the vision. The reports provide an overview of current knowledge, research, and debate for designers, users, and students. Other topics the book covers include: the virtual class online hypermedia; creating a community of learning using Web-based tools; multiuser discussion systems to support text-based virtual learning environments on the Internet; support for asynchronous collaborative knowledge work; use of Lotus Notes; the quality of use of multimedia learning systems; and the relevance and impact of collaborative management in a digital university.

◀ Hegarty, Michael, Ann Phelan, and Lisa Kilbride, eds. **Classrooms for Distance Teaching and Learning: A Blueprint**. Leuven, Belgium: Leuven University Press, 1998. ISBN 906168867X.

Administrators, faculty, and technical planners will find this handbook useful in setting up a classroom for telepresence learning. Chapters include steps for building an interactive classroom; testing how it works; using the classrooms for teachers, learners, tutors, facilitators, managers, and production/technical staff; and troubleshooting technical, audio, video, and network problems. The authors provide detailed case studies of the five distinctive learning scenarios, including sites for teaching remote and local learners, group presentation and interaction, a single learner, and a learning center group. A glossary, world TV standards, and list of Websites appear in the appendices.

◀ Moore, Michael, and Geoffrey T. Cozine, eds. **Web-Based Communications, The Internet, and Distance Education**. University Park, PA: The American Center for the Study of Distance Education, 2000. ISBN 1877780243.

In fairness to educators caught up in the new Web teaching and learning environment thrust upon them, there is a need to compare new ways of delivering instructions with former teaching and learning research, theory, and experiences. Moore and Cozine direct a number of criticisms at higher education institutions (e.g., their inability to develop Web-based instructional programs and thus keep up with the growth of technology); some educators and administrators are unwilling or unable to make the needed organizational and structural changes in their institution; and teachers may be reticent or unable to use the new technology and to apply it to teaching and learning methods.

◀ Moore, Michael G., and Namin Shin. **Speaking Personally About Distance Education**. University Park, PA: The American Center for the Study of Distance Education, 2000. ISBN 1877780235.

This book compiles 14 years of interviews with key distance learning founders from the United States and other countries. Informative interviews with college administrators and personalities from corporations, broadcasting, armed forces, and government discuss distance learning from its earliest forms to today's Web-based delivery of courses. These interviews were originally printed in the *American Journal of Distance Education*.

◀ Navarro, Peter, and Judy Shoemaker. **Performance and Perceptions of Distance Learners in Cyberspace**. In *Web-Based Communications, The Internet, and Distance Education*, ed. Michael Moore and Geoffrey T. Cozine, 1–15. University Park, PA: The American Center for the Study of Distance Education, 2000. ISBN 1877780243.

Navarro and Shoemaker present the results of a study of several hundred undergraduate students (cyberlearners) taking an economics course at the University of California. The authors evaluate the instructional technologies in use there, including CD-ROM-based lectures, electronic testing, threaded electronic bulletin boards, and online discussion rooms. They discuss teaching in cyberspace with regard to student performance, interaction, satisfaction, attitudes toward technology, and the efficacy of distance learning for educators and administrators.

◀ Peterman, Thomas W. **Elements of Success at a Traditional/Virtual University: Lessons Learned from Three Years of Growth in Cyberspace**. *Journal of Academic Librarianship* 26, no. 1 (2000): 27 (49 pars.). Online. EBSCOhost. *Academic Search Elite*. Article 2895265. (25 April 2001).

This case study reviews Park College's asynchronous distance learning program, which served more than 1,700 students per semester around the world. Through the collaboration of the administration, faculty, and a for-profit enterprise (V-Campus), the college provided academic services and support for students by using multiple formats of communication for the school's online courses. The authors discuss the needs of the administration and faculty, the profit/nonprofit perspective, benefits, accreditation, enrollments, and program quality. They hope that the experiences of this three-year collaborative venture will act as a model for other institutions.

◄ Petrides, Lisa A. **Web-Based Technologies for Distributed (or Distance) Learning: Creating Learning-Centered Educational Experiences in the Higher Education Classroom.** *International Journal of Instructional Media* 29, no.1 (2002): 69–77. (43 pars.). Online. *Ebsco Academic Elite* (Accession no. 6372446). (26 March 2002).

The author acknowledges that distributed learning (the use of Web-based technologies to supplement in-class teaching and learning) focuses on the delivery as the driving force in distance learning rather than focusing on learning-centered environments that are supported by the technology. Petrides conducted a graduate level educational administration course titled "Information Systems for Decision Making in Learning Organizations." Face-to-face classes were supplemented with LearningSpace—a Web-based software product consisting of four modules for scheduling, a media center, discussion rooms, and student profiles—and chat software called eShare Expressions to facilitate interaction between the student and the instructor. Petrides found that students valued a more learning-centered environment, where there was additional access to the ideas of other students and opportunities for collaboration, rather than a teacher-centered distributed learning environment. Original comments made by students in their evaluations are included in the study.

◄ Porter, Randall C. **Reaching Out.** *American School and University* 71, no. 12 (1999): 120–21.

This article discusses important considerations for designers of interactive distance learning classrooms. Porter describes in detail the interaction that takes place in a distant learning classroom (e.g., a camera at the podium replaces the blackboard or whiteboard; audiovisual materials are digitized and sent to projectors and monitors at both sites) and other important elements of this environment (e.g., zoned lighting; multidirectional microphones; cameras; cabling runs and raceways for power, data, and video; control booth; acoustical treatment for the walls; and staffing needs).

◄ Purdue, Kathy L., and Thomas Valentine. **Deterrents to Participating in Web-Based Continuing Professional Education.** In *Web-Based Communications, The Internet, and Distance Education*, ed. Michael Moore and Geoffrey T. Cozine, 24–38. University Park, PA: The American Center for the Study of Distance Education, 2000. ISBN 1877780243.

In this study, the authors sought to identify deterrents for certified public accountants who participated in Web-based continuing professional education. The study identifies four deterrent factors (e.g., issues of quality and electronically mediated communication for CPAs) that are of interest to administrators and policy makers who will be developing similar courses.

◀ Seagren, Alan T., and Sheldon L. Stick. **Enhancing Quality Through Distributed Education.** *Phi Delta Kappan* 80, no. 10 (1999): 793–94.

Seagren and Stick describe the development and implementation of a distributed doctoral program at the University of Nebraska. The technology for the program included adaptations of Lotus Notes, a groupware delivery system, and the Internet for students in Guam, Europe, and Nebraska. This virtual classroom facilitated energetic exchanges of information and multiple pathways to learning within each course. The communication among distributed course participants stands out as an excellent example of using new technology to ensure high-quality education. The program included a virtual cafeteria that served as a "meeting place" for discussion of course-related issues; a virtual faculty office for communication with faculty; the use of an electronic journal for students to make entries and collaborate with class members; a "literature bank" where students shared references, summaries, and even entire articles (when copyright was not an issue); and the "course library," a database embedded with all the required readings for a course, excluding the primary text.

◀ Smith, Sherri, and Andrea Benscoter. **Implementing an Internet Tutorial for Web-Based Courses.** In *Web-Based Communications, The Internet, and Distance Education*, ed. Michael Moore and Geoffrey T. Cozine, 131–36. University Park, PA: The American Center for the Study of Distance Education, 2000. ISBN 1877780243.

The authors describe the use of an Internet tutorial developed by the Florida Gulf Coast University to familiarize faculty and students with the technical aspects before taking a Web course. Of interest to faculty and administrators planning similar Web initiatives are the explanations the tutorial gives for such tasks as using e-mail, subscribing to a listserv, attaching documents to an e-mail, creating Word documents, accessing a Web board (bulletin board), exploring a university library's Website, and using a search engine.

◀ Spallek, Heiko, Peter Berthold, Diarmiud B. Shanley, and Rolf Attstrom. **Distance Education for Dentists: Improving the Quality of Online Instruction.** In *Web-Based Communications, The Internet, and Distance Education*, ed. Michael Moore and Geoffrey T. Cozine, 16–23. University Park, PA: The American Center for the Study of Distance Education, 2000. ISBN 1877780243.

In this study the authors provide quality assurance criteria for developing online dental education material and updated courses to meet the educational standards and goals of interest to the dental profession.

◀ Strong, Robert W., and E. Glynn Harmon. **Online Graduate Degrees: A Review of Three Internet-Based Master's Degree Offerings.** In *Web-Based Communications, The Internet, and Distance Education,* ed. Michael Moore and Geoffrey T. Cozine, 121–30. University Park, PA: The American Center for the Study of Distance Education, 2000. ISBN 1877780243.

The authors briefly examine three graduate programs (two offered through the Internet) and review the differences in each program's goals, the quality of information the programs provide, and potential problems for consumers (e.g., costs, accreditation, residency requirements, and sequel of coursework). Of interest to program planners wanting to guide potential students is the development of a list of questions by the authors titled "A Consumer's Guide to Online Degree Programs."

◀ Winer, Laura R., Martine Chomienne, and Jesus Vazquez-Abad. **A Distributed Collaborative Science Learning Laboratory on the Internet.** In *Web-Based Communications, The Internet, and Distance Education,* ed. Michael Moore and Geoffrey T. Cozine, 39–50. University Park, PA: The American Center for the Study of Distance Education, 2000. ISBN 1877780243.

The authors discuss the Electronic Circuit Simulator, a prototype developed to demonstrate the feasibility of a distributed collaborative science learning laboratory (DCSLL) for Internet-based collaborative learning for science courses. This model is of interest to science faculty who wish to provide authentic lab experiences and prevent students from feeling isolated.

Summary

In conclusion, the articles, books, and documents presented in this section barely touch the surface of the number of teaching and learning experiences that are taking place through Web-based instruction. It is vital for institutions to monitor the development of the new technologies for communicating through the Web, as well as the new software programs that help deliver instruction. Both administrators and faculty are equally involved in every aspect of Web-based instruction—from the development of the digital classroom to designs for Web-based programs or courses and their delivery to assessment of students' learning. The arrival of Web-based instruction not only radically changes both teaching and learning, but it also invites the formation of new models of providing education and new players that work alongside the traditional institutions of higher learning. This radical shift also brings with it the issues of maintaining quality, enrollment, and accreditation, as well as a number of education issues surrounding faculty and students. We address many of these topics in the section on administrative issues.

BROADCAST EDUCATION

Distance learning uses various technologies to create a virtual class-room. They range from a mailed document to the use of computers and broadcast media. These technologies must include a means of sending and receiving information and several ways to connect instructors and students. This section covers the use of broadcast televised programs such as telecourses, interactive TV, teleconferencing, and videoconferencing. Each of these modes brings with it its own concerns that involve technology requirements and challenges for students, instructors, and administrators. Related articles describing these issues follow a brief description of each mode of transmission.

Telecourses

Public broadcasting and some commercial radio and television stations provide courses on a regular schedule so that classroom instructors can tune in at predetermined times. These telecourses reach a wider audience and are accessible to many students or a single student at one time. Videotaped telecourses are limited to the time and place of the broadcast. Broadcast programs involve the senses of hearing and sight. Interaction between students and teachers is limited, and production of these telecourses requires a recording talent, studio recording time, and airtime.

The literature on the use of telecourses in distance learning indicates there are more limitations than benefits as a means of distance learning. Telecourses are packaged, semester-long courses that combine televised lessons with textbooks, study guides, and other written material. A telecourse is different from a "teleclass," in which a given lecture is taped and transmitted in real time over cable or satellite networks to students watching either in other classrooms or at home. A telecourse is also different from an "interactive teleclass," in which students and faculty in classrooms at multiple sights are linked in real time by a combination of video and audio. Telecourses can be an excellent tool for providing information; the danger is that they can also become "canned" material and pedagogy that will quickly become outdated.[13] Other limitations are that, by their very nature, they are one-way (noninteractive) and thus will never promote the consistent group learning that sparks critical thinking.[14] When instructors and designers plan telecourses to fill the need of distance learning, it is a good idea to promote learning communities that somehow enable learners to interact face-to-face in study groups or at a distance through e-mail, a listserv, or an electronic bulletin board.[15] The following quote reflects an administrator's point of view about the loss of the live interaction between professors and their students that is crucial to the academic experience.

The challenge for policy-makers and the general public is to resist the impulse to force colleges and universities into substituting the kind of rote training that technology can cheaply supply for the more expensive education that teaches critical thinking and analytic skills, values and an understanding of complex relationships, which the learned professor in the classroom can facilitate. An exclusively cost-driven dependence on computers and telecourses may instruct students in a subject, but only a professor with passion and disciplinary expertise can help students understand why a subject is important to think about and how to think about it.[16]

◀ Weigand, Kathy. **Adult Learners and Distance Education Evaluation: Implications for Success.** Miami: Barry University, 2000. ERIC, ED 441081.

Weigand's report evaluates an adult degree distance education program delivered as a telecourse through a public television station. She examines both positive and negative student responses obtained from questionnaires relating to their motivation, independent learning style, discipline, time management, organization, study habits, reading comprehension, exam taking, procrastination, tenacity, responsibility for learning, satisfaction with the course, opinion about whether they would register for another similar course, and future courses they would like to see offered. For administrators and program planners considering the use of telecourses, the need for interaction stands out as an important aspect of the learning process that is lacking in this medium.

Interactive Television

◀ Anderson, Lorraine P., Steven R. Banks, and Paul A. Leary. **The Effect of Interactive Television Courses on Student Satisfaction.** *Journal of Education for Business* (January/February 2002): 164–68. (34 pars.). Online. Ebsco Academic Elite (Accession no. 6380525). (26 March 2002).

This research study helps administrators decide if ITV (interactive television) courses warrant the expense of developing an ITV delivery system for distance learning. The authors review recent research that discusses the benefits of ITV to remote students and compares students' outcomes and instructors' communication for the traditional on-campus student with that for remote students. Because of the lack of research in this area, the authors focus this study on student satisfaction.

The study of more than 3,000 students at Marshall University in Huntington, West Virginia compared student evaluations for both on-site and remote ITV instruction. It found significantly lower student course satisfaction for students taught at remote sites. The results of this study alert administrators to two important findings: (1) the importance of student satisfaction with regard to developing programs using ITV delivery systems; and (2) that students' frustration with ITV delivery systems may have influenced their overall opinion of the instructor and the instructor's presentation style, thus resulting in poorer instructor evaluations that could have an effect on tenure decisions.

◀ Giglio, Rob. **The Story Behind HDTV**. *Media and Methods* 36, no. 3 (January/February 2000): 31.

Giglio describes a standardized high definition television (HDTV) signal that all major broadcasters such as network, cable, and satellite companies will use by the year 2006. Of interest to educators is the fact that the superior pictures from HDTV will project an almost three-dimensional-like picture that will enhance demonstrations and lessons for teaching. For example, Giglio explains that the quality of HDTV screens will make a distant instructor appear more real. Three other participating remote classrooms will appear on the same screen at the same time. Although HDTV is costly and still in its infancy, professionals in the field predict that prices will fall, making it more available. The use of HDTV is promising, and it will provide new and better opportunities for the medium of television to improve the distance learning environment.

◀ Mottet, Timothy P. **Teaching from a Distance: "Hello, Is Anyone out There?"** Paper presented at the Annual Ethnography in Research Forum, Philadelphia, 6 March 1998. ERIC, ED 417436.

Mottet investigated learning outcomes for students in an electronically mediated environment that uses interactive television (ITV). This report on his study provides a list of questions and recommendations made by instructors that can be helpful to others using interactive television. Examples of the questions are the following: What happens to the teachers' verbal and nonverbal messages when they are mediated? What happens to teacher–student interaction? How does a teacher regulate interaction in an environment where the verbal and nonverbal cues remain filtered or dulled? Are we creating virtual classrooms because we should or because we can? Should we not expect learning outcomes in the virtual classroom to exceed those in the traditional classroom?

◀ Paterson, Wendy A. **Distance Learning: Up Close and Personal**. *TechTrends* 43, no. 6 (December 1999): 20–25.

Paterson describes an interactive television distance learning model, Project Jump Start, which was initiated in the fall of 1995 at Buffalo State

College in New York. ITV courses were taught to college and high school students in 14 undergraduate courses and funded through a cooperative arrangement between Bell Atlantic and the Center for Applied Research in Interactive Technologies (CARIT). Paterson provides the reader with a reflective account of her own personal experience, how her teaching style evolved, student outcomes, and some of the challenges and difficulties she and her students encountered. She also describes for faculty and administrators a variety of teaching and assessment techniques. The key to the success of ITV is the provision of funding by an outside source—an important issue for making ITV available for distance learning.

Teleconferencing

Teleconferencing uses electronic communications between two or more participants who are in separate locations. Teleconferencing enables teachers to present—on television screens in remote locations—information that is uplinked and downlinked, sometimes via satellite, and it allows one- or two-way audio or audiovisual communication between students and teachers. Participants can see what is taking place at the site where the transmission is originating and interact with people at the originating and linked sites.[17] However, teleconferencing is limited in the times and places it may occur. It also may be videotaped for later use. Teleconferencing requires a videoconferencing system, including monitors, cameras, fiber-optic cable connections, a specially equipped classroom, and visual tools to supplement the videoconferencing system, such as a slide-to-video, scan converter for the PC, a DVD player, a VCR, a document camera, one or more "face" or "people" cameras and microphones, and display devices such as video monitors or plasma screens.[18]

Desktop Videoconferencing

Desktop videoconferencing involves one student or a group of students at one time. It can link participants working at stand-alone computers, enabling them to see and hear each other. Because desktop videoconferencing makes use of individual computers, each unit must be equipped with a camera to show who is working at that computer.[19] Participants may be able to send e-mail to each other during the videoconference and share online documents. There may be a limit to the times and places for the videoconference. It allows one- or two-way audio or audiovisual communication between students and teachers. It requires videoconferencing capability, including computers and software for sending and receiving multimedia information, and connection to a local area network (LAN) or a wide area network (WAN).

Teleconferences and videoconferences are widely used forms of distance learning. A two-way teleconference among people at remote locations by means of transmitted audio and video signals can also take place. Instructors and students use these effective forms of distance learning face to face through computers and telephonic technology. Teleconferences and videoconferences require students to see demonstrations, participate in discussions, listen to lectures, view presentations, and work in groups. They may be the only methods of transmitting information for a distance learning course. Students must participate in the teleconference, which may take place once or several times a week, as is expected through a traditional class experience. The teleconferencing and videoconferencing modes of distance learning mimic some of the elements of traditional classroom education while providing other educational opportunities. Students may have access to professional gatherings, demonstrations, and workshops hosted by a professional or business group. Teleconferences and videoconferences can also enhance other instructional methods.

Teleconferencing and desktop videoconferencing provide a forum for discussion and a way to share materials gathered in the course or discuss projects. Students or groups of students link to a discussion and see the presentation of educational material in real time. Teleconferences provide instruction to individuals or several groups of learners at one time. Videoconferencing links individuals (with limits on the number of participants who can be linked at one time). In that participants meet at a specified time and location, the course is highly structured.

Distance learning programs may involve additional methods of distributing instruction such as hardcopy documents, audiotapes, videotapes, disks, CDs, broadcasts, and e-mail, used alone or in combination. Surface mail correspondence, the older and slower method of distribution, may include print, video, audio, and disk materials that teachers may easily copy. Hardcopy requires printing or reproduction and mailing. Audiotape limits instruction that students can hear; however, it may not be useful to students with special needs. There is little interaction with the instructor or group at the same time. Audiotapes require a recording talent, recording of a master soundtrack, duplication of tapes, and a mailing or delivery. Videotapes may be easily copied. There is little interaction with the instructor, and they may be used by an individual or a group at the same time. Videotaping requires a recording talent, taping and editing of a master copy, and duplication of tapes. Mailing or deliveries are possible. E-mail correspondence is potentially a faster method of distribution but is limited to students with access to e-mail and an e-mail account. E-mail may include attached documents and graphics and may be distributed to many students at once or to a single student. E-mail promotes frequent communication among students and instructors.

A Website includes the use of hypertext and hypermedia materials. Websites are potentially the faster method of distribution. Students must have access to the Internet. A single student or many students may access the Web at once and may include e-mail ("mailto") links. Teachers update the Website frequently and may install security measures to limit access to students. There is limited instantaneous interaction between students and instructors. Access to a Website requires the use of a computer, the Internet, and a Web browser and user fees. The following section provides an in-depth description of Web-based instruction and a review of the literature.

Teleconferencing/Videoconferencing

◀ Bivens, Herbert L., and Alan Chute. **Distance Learning Futures: Creating New Learning Environments and Developing New Pedagogical Skills.** URL: http://www.al.lu/videoconf/edu01.html (4 April 2002).

Bivens and Chute explore the technological potential and use of desktop and group videoconferencing systems that provide two-way video and heightened interactivity between professor and student. The authors identify excellent guidelines and suggestions for educators to use in developing the most conducive distance learning environment. They stress the importance of the physical learning environment and the pedagogical skills the instructor employs in distance learning programs. Bivens and Chute state:

> Having the right video teleconferencing technology in place is only half the story; skillfully presenting a relevant learning experience that is well organized, appropriate to the learning context and very interactive is essential to enable the learner to achieve their goals and expected outcomes. (6)

◀ Crook, Robert, and Thomas Cyrs. **Using Distance Learning to Teach at a Distance: How to Survive and Thrive in a Satellite Teleconference.** Paper presented at the Annual Conference on Distance Teaching and Learning '99, University of Wisconsin-Madison, August 1999. ERIC, ED 440287.

Crook and Cyrs describe a teleconference, "Creative Teaching at a Distance with the Merging Technologies," that was developed specifically to demonstrate how to teach at a distance through this medium. They outline key elements for designing a high-quality teleconference, personnel requirements, and needed equipment. Planners will also benefit by reviewing the detailed account of the steps that went into the planning and execution of the teleconference.

◀ Dolhon, James P. **Multi-Point Videoconferencing As Collaborative Co-Productions (Part II).** *Distant Education* 3, no. 3 (March 1999): 2–3.

This article discusses teaching methods used in a videoconference environment. This review—aimed at institutions—focuses on the technical aspects of setting up a conference (e.g., a voice-activation microphone, split-screen) and the effectiveness of this mode of instruction.

◀ Hackmann, Donald G., and James E. Berry. **Distance Learning in Educational Administration Doctoral Programs: The Wave of the Future?** *Journal of School Leadership* 9, no. 4 (July 1999): 349–67. FirstSearch ERIC (Accession no. EJ589448). (11 May 2000).

The results of a survey involving more than 100 doctoral, educational administration institutions reveal that half of these use distance learning through interactive video and the Internet. The study also discuses issues such as faculty workload, costs, and the quality of these programs for administrators.

◀ Omatseye, J. Nesin. **Teaching Through Tele-conferencing: Some Curriculum Challenges.** *College Student Journal* 33, no. 3 (September 1999): 346–53.

In this article Omatseye provides the reader with an excellent description of teleconferencing as a means to distance learning and a brief history of how it has developed since its inception in the early 1980s in Kentucky. He describes Eastern Kentucky University's Tele-Linking Network (KTLN), which connects students to its faculty, classrooms, and equipment. Helpful to planners are a description of the cost benefits of interactive television and the results of a survey given to students indicating their reservations and endorsements. The author also provides a detailed list of tips and teleteaching strategies for institutions and instructors.

◀ Payne, Hank. **A Review of the Literature: Interactive Video Teletraining in Distance Learning Courses.** United States Distance Learning Association, 2000. URL: http://www.usdla.org/PDF_files/Review_of_Literature.pdf (15 August 2001).

Payne presents a collection of important research studies on interactive videoteletraining for distance learning. The review of the literature covers the four-year period from 1994 to 1998. The studies focus on learner achievement, learner satisfaction, the use of student response systems (e.g., voice and data capabilities), and interaction in instructional television courses delivered at a distance. Payne introduces each section with a description of the topic. The topics are followed by a review of over 800 research studies. This document (a doctoral dissertation) provides a comprehensive summary of the latest research in this area. Institutions that are involved in this medium of distance learning or those contemplating it will find this information helpful.

◄ Reis, Raul, Alan G. Stravitsky, Tim Gleason, and William Ryan. **Journalism at a Distance: The Oregon Experiment.** *Journalism and Mass Communication Educator* 54, no. 4 (Winter 2000): 14–28 (90 pars.). Online. Proquest. (25 April 2001).

After receiving a grant, journalism professors were able to use the Oregon telecommunication network to deliver the journalism school's introductory courses to colleges throughout Oregon. This article describes this distance education project that used real-time video, audio hook-up videoconferencing technology, and computer access to remote locations. The authors discuss the stages of the project, the technological and structural issues, and the project's achievements and analyze valuable political, economic, bureaucratic, and pedagogical issues for other institutions.

◄ Reynolds, Sally, Gee Cammaert, and Johan Van Heddegem. **Success Factors in Telepresence Teaching: Results from the Blueprint for Interactive Classrooms (BIC) Project Involving European Universities.** Paper presented at the Annual Conference on Distance Teaching and Learning '99, University of Wisconsin-Madison, August 1999. ERIC, ED 440287.

A consortium of universities in Belgium, Finland, France, Ireland, and Italy experienced in using videoconferencing built five telepresence teaching sites. The purpose of this project was to further explore synchronous telepresence teaching using a variety of media, to design a range of interactive telepresence classrooms, and to produce products for other institutions and training organizations that want to begin their own programs. The authors describe the "Blueprint for Interactive Classrooms" project, in which classrooms are designed for a number of teaching and learning scenarios (e.g., an area suited to group presentations and interaction or a learning area for a single learner). Of interest to institutions planning to develop similar projects is the availability of an excellent handbook created from the project. The handbook contains illustrations, checklists, glossaries, and diagrams that administrators and technicians can use to set up their own facility. The URL is http://www.linov.kuleuven.ac.be/BIC.

◄ Spence, Lundie, Harriett S. Stubbs, and Richard A. Huber. **TelEE: A Description of an Interactive Telecommunication Course.** *T.H.E. Journal* 28, no. 2 (Sept 2000): 24–31.

The authors discuss the planning and evaluation of the environmental education course TelEE, designed by faculty from four North Carolina campuses. The North Carolina Research and Education Network (NC-REN) Interactive Video Services is a multisite, multichannel, interactive network that connects more than 19 universities, medical schools, and research organizations that offer credit courses, continuing education, conferences, and interactive seminars. The authors describe the circumstances that created the need for TelEE, ways in which the technologies facilitated collaboration and inter-action, the role of assessment of students, and the course itself. For planners and faculty they also list several keys to success.

◄ Weedman, Judith. **Conversation and Community: The Potential of Electronic Conferences for Creating Intellectual Proximity in Distributed Learning Environments.** *Journal of the American Society for Information Science* 50, no. 10 (August 1999): 907–28. OCLC FirstSearch ERIC (Accession no. EJ 591689).

This report reviews teleconferencing as a form of distance learning for graduate students. As a tool for administrators and faculty considering this medium of distance learning, the author reviews the literature and discusses outcomes and the relationships and professional socialization of students.

Electronic Mail

The use of e-mail as a form of computer-mediated communication has grown considerably, bringing with it many challenges to human communication. E-mail discussions are asynchronous (time and place independent) and simple to use. E-mail also provides an opportunity for giving class assignments and serves as a forum for questions and answers between students and professors. It can be used for many purposes and has many benefits including the fostering of a strong sense of community.[20] Other forms of computer-mediated communication include the use of online chat and bulletin board tools that supplement face-to-face communication.

◄ Becker, Ellen A. **Implementing an Interdisciplinary Module Through Computer Conferencing.** Paper presented at the Annual Conference on Distance Teaching and Learning '99, University of Wisconsin-Madison, August 1999. ERIC, ED 440287.

Becker describes the planning, implementation, evaluation, and out-comes of developing a course for students from various health professions. WebBoard (computing conferencing software) was used in developing a plan of care in conjunction with a patient's history. Becker describes the techno-logical difficulties experienced, as well as problems with student participa-tion. She provides a list of lessons learned that will help facilitate such initiatives by other institutions.

◀ Marttunen, Muka, and Leena Laurinen. **Argumentative Interaction in an Academic E-Mail Course.** Paper presented as part of Networked Learning 2000: Innovative Approaches to Lifelong Learning and Higher Education Through the Internet, International Conference, Lancaster, England, 17–19 April 2000. England: Department of Educational Studies. ERIC, ED 441078.

Marttunen and Laurinen describe how e-mail was used in a 10-week course at a Finnish university—The University of Jyvaskyla—to develop students' argumentation skills at the university level. Their study is only one example of the value of using e-mail to help develop students' communication skills through the Internet. However, the authors advise that additional studies will be needed to evaluate the use of e-mail as a communication tool for other purposes.

One hopes that the descriptions of various forms of broadcast methods provide a distinction between these methods of distance education delivery and Web-based instruction methods. A sampling of the literature describes these delivery methods and reveals the issues associated with them. Institutions and faculty need to continue to monitor the literature and consider the relevant issues for their roles as administrators or educators.

NOTES

1.   Moore, Michael, and Geoffrey T. Cozine, eds. *Web-Based Communications, The Internet, and Distance Education.* University Park, PA: The American Center for the Study of Distance Education, 2000. ISBN 1877780243.

2.   Bradshaw, D. H., and K. Desser. *Audiographics Distance Learning: A Resource Handbook.* San Francisco: Far West Laboratory for Educational Research and Development, 1990; available from the following Website: http://www.dlrn.org/library/glossary/audiographics.html (4 April 2002).

3.   Ibid.

4.   "Distance Learning Glossary." Distance Learning Resource Network; available from the following Website: http://www.dlrn.org/library/glossary (26 March 2002).

5.   Porter, Lynnette R. *Creating the Virtual Classroom: Distance Learning with the Internet.* New York: John Wiley, 1997, 24. ISBN 0471178306.

6.   Reza Hazemi, Stephen Hailes, and Steve Wilbur. *The Digital University: Reinventing the Academy.* London, Great Britain: Springer-Verlag, 2001, 56. ISBN 1852334789.

7.   Davis, J. Duke Finds Virtual Classrooms Teach Communication. *InfoWorld* [online magazine] (8 February 1999); Expanded Academic Index (Article no. A53745223).

8.   Svetcov, Danielle. The Virtual Classroom vs. the Real One. *Forbes* 166, no. 7 (2000): 50–53.

9.   Clayton, Mark. Learning: Colleges and Universities: Click 'n' Learn. *The Christian Science Monitor* 92, no. 185 (August 2000): 20–21.

10.   Daniel, Sir John. Medium and Message: Passion, Values, and Quality in the New Academy. In *Higher Education 2000: What Will Be New? What Will Be Different? Proceedings of AQA '99,* 1999. Philadelphia: Middle States Commission on Higher Education, 2000, 14.

11.   Ibid., 15.

12.   Whiteman, Jo Ann. *Learning Environment for the Next Generation.* ERIC, ED 441158.

13.   Accetta, Randy. TV Teachers and Regurgitation: The Implications of Using Telecourses to Teach English Studies. Paper presented at the Forty-Ninth Annual Meeting of the Conference on College Composition and Communication, Chicago. 1–4 April 1998. ERIC, ED 426410.

14.   Ibid.

15.   Eagan, Winston M., and Gordon S. Gibb. Student Centered Instruction for the Design of Telecourses. In "Teaching and Learning at a Distance: What It Takes to Effectively Design, Deliver, and Evaluate Programs." *New Directions for Teaching and Learning* no. 71 (Fall 1997). San Francisco: Jossey-Bass. ISBN 0787998842.

16.   Kolodny, Annette. *Failing the Future: A Dean's Look at Higher Education in the Twenty-First Century.* Durham: Duke University Press, 1998. ISBN 0822321866.

17.   Porter, Lynnette R. *Creating the Virtual Classroom: Distance Learning with the Internet.* New York: John Wiley, 1997. ISBN 0471178306.

18.   Sharer, Scott. Videoconferencing and Distance Learning. *Media and Methods* 37, no. 2 (November/December 2000): 6.

19.   Porter, 1997.

20.   Bruce-Hyter, Catherine. Computer Mediated Communication in Graduate Distance Education: A Qualitative Case Study. Master's thesis, Memorial University of Newfoundland, 1997. ISBN 0612175731.

Administrative Issues for Higher Education

Throughout the literature on distance learning numerous issues that higher education institutions need to address continually surface. These issues include the planning, developing, and marketing of distance learning and the evaluation of its effectiveness. A challenging task for institutions is that drawing students nationally or internationally requires a successful marketing or advertising campaign.[1] Budgetary concerns range from the projected costs of running a distance learning program to the question of who controls the budget, the cost of salaries, and fringe benefits for administrators, faculty, and other professionals, clerical help, and student labor. The tuition rate or special tuition for distance learning students, a support structure to help users (24 hours a day, 7 days a week), and student services are expensive. For example, "a university help desk servicing 1,000 online students per year can cost almost $300,000 and require up to eleven employees."[2] There is also the cost of developing online courses. "The costs for course development can range from a few hundred to millions of dollars."[3] Marketing distant education programs is another major expense. "The global education market today is $2 trillion dollars. The current very small online education share will grow to $15 billion dollars by 2002, according to the International Data Corporation information technology analysts."[4] Other major costs include the development of an infrastructure and facilities; a high-speed network and new distance learning technologies; operational support—supplies, telephone, heating, electricity, insurance, maintenance, and so on; furniture for the classroom; and office equipment—computers, transmission equipment, copiers, and facsimile machines.

Concerns about the organizational structure center around who will carry out the mission and purposes of the project. Are there new administrative jobs? Who does the administrator for the distance education project report to? Technology issues include deciding on which transmission technology to use. Will distance learning be carried out through the use of cable, satellite, two-way video, course-in-a-box (open learning) through Web-based courses, multimedia courses using computer, e-mail, videoconferencing, audioconferencing, Internet Relay Chat (IRC), CD-ROM, textbooks, or some future mode of transmission? "There is also a bewildering variety of software, hardware, ancillary services, and advice, much of which is marketed without full testing and on the basis of an entrepreneur's best guess."[5]

What about accreditation and issues of regulation? How do the governing accreditation bodies decide who to accredit? Institutions that have developed distance learning programs and those considering moving into this area need to address academic issues such as faculty attitudes, compensation, ownership of materials, training, and evaluation; student enrollment, registration, advising, assessment, financial aid, support resources, and learning outcomes; and access to entire degree or ad hoc courses and the location of these courses—via the Internet, over cable, or at a local high school, an off-campus center, or some other location. Other issues pertain to the competition from virtual colleges and universities that do not have a traditional campus.

To review these concerns as well as others, this section cites published papers, reports, and surveys presented at conferences, Websites, or information from institutions themselves as they began offering distance education.

PLANNING

◀ Chisholm, Wendy. **Creating Accessible Content for the World Wide Web and Distance Education.** Paper presented at the Annual Conference on Distance Teaching and Learning '99, University of Wisconsin-Madison, August 1999. ERIC, ED 440287.

Chisholm provides valuable information regarding Internet accessibility to people with disabilities. This information is extremely important for faculty or Web developers who design the content for Web courses. Chisholm describes the development of courseware products that help students use the Web effectively. This timely paper tries to address a large population that we must not forget in the rush to move to distance education through the World Wide Web. Chisholm reports that in April 1997, the World Wide Web Consortium (W3C) (http://www.w3.org) launched a Web Accessibility Initiative (WAI) (http://www.w3.org/WAI), which is an international group of people working together to foster the development of new technologies.

◀ Chute, Alan G., and Herbert L. Bivens. **Ten Tips for Implementing a Distance Learning Program**. http://www.usoe.k12.ut.us/curr/ednet /training/resources/ednetRes/10Steps.pdf (4 April 2002).

Chute and Bivens provide an excellent list of tips for institutions that are implementing a distance learning program for interactive video or videoconferencing. The authors discuss the marketing of such a program, the need for well-trained instructors, the design of the program, and the necessary equipment.

◀ **Distance Learning Enrollments in Independent Institutions: Feasibility Study**. Olympia: State of Washington Higher Education Coordinating Board, 1999. ERIC, ED 441381.

This report reviews issues affecting the feasibility of collecting distance learning data through the use of surveys. Although the report provides an enlightening look at the diverse growth of distance learning, the information the surveys recorded revealed less than encouraging data. This study clearly points out the need for administrators to follow the research on distance learning, to study the experiences of other institutions, and to examine the data before jumping on the bandwagon and investing in distance learning programs that may or may not be beneficial. The study also points out the need for accrediting and educational agencies to devise a plan that will compile data to help guide institutions that are interested in participating in distance learning.

◀ Galusha, Jill. **Barriers to Learning in Distance Education**. University of Southern Mississippi. http://www.infrastruction.com/barriers .htm (August 2001).

Galusha describes the various types of distance education and the barriers (e.g., motivation, feedback and teacher contact, support services, alienation, and lack of experience and training) faced by students, faculty, and the sponsoring organization. Knowing the problems and learning to overcome them involves a collaborative effort of administration, faculty, and technical support staff in a distance learning program that is necessary to achieve success. Doing this requires thorough planning.

◀ Halliwell, Julian. **As Simple As Possible, As Complex As Necessary: An Approach to the Design and Development of Web-Based Learning Environments**. Paper presented at the Networked Learning 2000: Innovative Approaches to Lifelong Learning and Higher Education Through the Internet, International Conference, Lancaster, England, 17–19 April 2000. ERIC, ED 441078.

Halliwell cautions both educational and technical developers of Internet-based learning not to lose sight of the students' needs for simplicity and user-friendly features. They should also become familiar with online teaching and learning issues when designing teaching exercises. Interfaces should be simple to use, functional, and both internally and externally consistent. "There is a tendency to place greater importance on developing 'cutting edge' functionality without considering fully whether the resulting systems are appropriate or will ultimately be effective" (122).

The author recommends that Web designers take into account learning styles, accommodations for students with disabilities, course content, and the social aspect of interaction. His paper offers practical advice for administrators, faculty, and Web designers who must collaborate when developing the Web teaching and learning environment.

◀ Munkittrick, Peggy. **Building a Foundation for Connected Learning**. *T.H.E. Journal* 27, no. 9 (April 2000): 54–56.

Munkittrick lists six elements that administrators and educators must deal with in order to build an effective distance learning environment and then provides detailed information on them. These elements include: (1) network infrastructure and support; (2) an administrative system's seamless data flow; (3) customized portals (to access course content and resources, reporting and grades, and collaborative learning tools); (4) tools for content development and course management; (5) learning object repositories—a searchable library for learning objects such as lectures or slide presentations; and (6) an integrator to take course content from the virtual world into the administrative world.

◀ Reddi, Usha, and Anita Dighe. **Literacy and Adult Education Through Distance and Open Learning**. In *Basic Education at a Distance: World Review of Distance Education and Open Learning*, vol. 2, ed. Chris Yates and Jo Bradley, 155–72. New York: Routledge/ Farmer, 2000. ISBN 0415237734.

The authors examine case studies revolving around the debate of literacy and adult education for distance learners, and they report on the implications for learners and their literacy needs. They suggest that planners and educators look beyond literacy to the provision of equitable access to distance learning to everyone.

◀ Thompson, John M., and Connie Broughton. **How Do You Plan, Develop, and Implement a Statewide Virtual Community College in One Year?** Paper presented at the Annual Conference on Distance Teaching and Learning '99, University of Wisconsin-Madison, August 1999. ERIC, ED 440287.

Thompson and Broughton describe the efforts of 32 Washington state community and technical colleges to plan, develop, and implement a statewide virtual community college brought about by students' demands for online education. They also discuss the ability of any one school to finance such a venture independently. This paper is helpful for other institutions seeking to develop a virtual college because it gives a good description of management issues, criteria, and standards for developing courses and questions to consider when selecting a vendor to provide support for the technology infrastructure.

NEED FOR DISTANCE LEARNING

Distance learning has evolved through the centuries from a bricks-and-mortar tradition, in which students received degrees from an established university (first generation), to the present generation, in which open learning universities (mega-universities) use a variety of distance learning technologies. The future and third generation will experience the virtual university and the emerging mega-universities with staff and students drawn from global networks.[6] "The Internet is not simply another technological advance that can be responded to in a typical way; it is a 'set of transforming technologies' that impact both the care of the educational processes of institutions and the fundamental competitive forces institutions face. It impacts the way students can access higher education and the way teaching and learning can take place, and significantly changes the competitive landscape for almost all institutions."[7]

In much of the literature one statement that is heard again and again is that higher education is now undergoing and will continue to undergo profound structural changes. Two significant reasons for bringing about this change arise from the technology. Whatever is digitally delivered to a user will change and may even displace what cannot be delivered. For example, new learning modalities such as instruction that is mediated may not totally displace instructors; it will, however, change where and how they will work. For institutions, the cost and cost-effectiveness factor will also be deemed more important than the quality of teaching.[8] Traditionally, higher education both in the United States and abroad has been the provider of knowledge, but that is changing in today's educational technologic environment. As Castells states, "Universities do not seem to have emerged as the central institutions of postindustrial society. Corporations (public and private), hospitals, and health care systems, school systems, and the media are such central institutions, deeply transformed by the intensive use of new information and communications technologies."[9] The new millennium will see the extent of this paradigm shift and will witness the extent to which traditional universities adapt, reshape themselves, or are eliminated.[10] The following articles, papers, and so on further discuss these changes and trends that higher education must heed.

◀ Green, Kenneth C. **When Wishes Come True: Colleges and the Convergence of Access, Lifelong Learning, and Technology.** *Change* 31, no. 2 (1999): 10–15.

Green reviews the issues faced by faculty and information technology (IT) instruction. He discusses content, delivery, and infrastructure as the three key issues for IT-based instruction. Green provides a fresh look at what colleges usually state as their mission (research and scholarship, teaching and learning, and public service) and puts a new focus on an instructional mission that involves three primary functions—content (what is taught), context (the environment that fosters or supports instruction and learning), and certification (documenting outcomes). This article dispels the predictions that distance learning will bring about the demise of the traditional campus. Instead, the author offers an understanding of what higher education needs to do to grow through this new revolution.

◀ Lundin, Roy. **Being Unreal: Epistemology, Ontology, and Phenomenology in a Virtual Educational World.** In *Web-Based Communications, The Internet, and Distance Education*, ed. Michael Moore and Geoffrey T. Cozine, 100–108. University Park, PA: The American Center for the Study of Distance Education, 2000. ISBN 1877780243.

In this essay Lundin examines philosophical questions surrounding teaching and learning in the virtual world of the Internet against the backdrop of H. G. Wells's 1938 book *World Brain/World Mind*. Lundin predicts that this new era of global distance learning will lead to new forms of information literacy.

◀ MacDonald, Gerard. **Universities and Knowledge Economies: A Paradigmatic Change?** Unpublished paper. Networked Learning 2000: Innovative Approaches to Lifelong Learning and Higher Education Through the Internet, April 2000. *Proceedings of the International Conference*, Lancaster, Sheffield University. ERIC, ED 441078.

MacDonald's paper makes for interesting reading for administrators, technical personnel, and faculty alike in higher education because it describes the scenarios affecting the very face of higher education. Institutions of higher education will not be the only players in the distance learning arena, and that is why it is very important for them to look carefully at the signs of change around them as they make plans for the twenty-first century.

Some of MacDonald's predictions are listed here:

- Teaching programs will be globally networked;
- Institutional frontiers will erode, e.g., researchers can invent anything, anywhere;

- The combination of transparency and connectivity will change universities' internal structures and dissolve discipline boundaries;

- Collaboration across disciplines or geographic borders will raise the question of institutional ownership;

- Technology will change the boundaries within universities as many new partnerships develop;

- Businesses will seek to influence university teaching;

- The state will scrutinize its higher education institutions financially;

- Corporations will individually assess a university's courses and departments before supporting employees taking them;

- Teaching standards and evaluations will become stricter; and

- Commercial competition will bring about a deregulation of academia.

◀ Oblinger, Diana G., and Mark K. Maruyama. **Distributed Learning.** Boulder, CO: CAUSE, 1999.

In this paper Oblinger and Maruyama discuss ways in which administrators and faculty in higher education must deal with new approaches to course and curriculum design, rethink conventional methods of course development, and creat affordable and flexible student-centered distributed learning environments that differ from the traditional teacher-centered classrooms. The authors review long-standing educational practices (e.g., teachers lecture while students listen) and preferred educational practices (e.g., teacher as a guide, coach, motivator, and facilitator).

◀ Senta, T. Della, and F. T. Tschang, eds. **Access to Knowledge: New Information Technologies and the Emergence of the Virtual University**, vol. 16. New York: Elsevier Science, 2000. ISBN 0080436706.

This book focuses on the growth of technology on the Web and the emergence of virtual universities, ways in which these developments are transforming the roles and organizational structure of educational systems, and the issues and concerns (such as costs) of institutions and technology systems. The book also examines learning, new pedagogy, curricula, and learning activities. The content is informative and essential for administrators, faculty, planners, and policy makers.

◀ Teare, Richard, David Davies, and Eric Sandelands. **The Virtual University: An Action Paradigm and Process for Workplace Learning**. New York: Continuum International Publishing Group, 1999. ISBN 0304703273.

◀ Van Der Molen, H. J., ed. **Virtual University? Educational Environments for the Future**. Princeton: Princeton University Press, 2000. ISBN 185578145X.

Stressing the need for institutions to change their patterns of teaching and learning, these essays caution that unless these changes occur, institutions are in danger of shrinking or disappearing. The book's message is meant for all who are involved in teaching and learning, as well as those who manage educational systems. The writers who contributed to this book discuss open distance learning, virtual universities, models for Web-based education, communication technologies, assessment, learning styles, and challenges for the future.

◀ Werry, Chris, and Miranda Mowbray. **Online Communities: Commerce, Community Action, and the Virtual University**. Paramus, NJ: Prentice Hall, 2000. ISBN 0130323829.

The authors provide examples of leading models of online communities in education, commerce, the nonprofit sector, and distance learning. Experts from these communities discuss the uses of these models and issues that evolve from them.

MARKETING

◀ Finkelstein, Martin J., Carol Frances, Frank I. Jewett, and Bernhard W. Scholz, eds. 296–313. **Dollars, Distance, and Online Education: The New Economics of College Teaching and Learning**. Phoenix: Oryx Press, 2000. ISBN 1573563951.

This book offers advice from IT experts, administrators, and faculty based on their experiences with developing the technology infrastructure for the Internet in higher education. These valuable shared experiences help to guide other institutions' economic and planning decisions.

The chapter by Goldberg and Seldin explains the reasons that higher education institutions need to take a more businesslike approach for the future when it comes to planning, developing, funding, and marketing online ventures. They list the major categories of expenditures and suggest a percentage of the total budget for each that can act as a guideline for others facing these decisions.

The remaining chapters in this book address other issues as well. With regard to budgeting and marketing, the chapter by Boettcher outlines the steps planners must take in order to move a course to the Web (e.g., budgetary concerns, resources, and the time needed for developing courses).

The chapter by Eggins shares the results of a survey that examines the costs of technology-based education at institutions of higher learning in the United Kingdom, Canada, Europe, and Australia. The studies presented in this chapter act as a valuable source of information for institutions in the United States and offer an opportunity to compare costs with other institutions. Eggins promotes the idea of global collaboration in order for institutions to make the most efficient use of their financial resources.

Green's chapter explains the cost significance of IT on a campus as more than computer and technical resources or instructional technology that enhances teaching and learning. Green discusses the lack of both investment policy and funding for the operating and infrastructure costs on campuses.

The chapter by Jewett analyzes the costs of classroom instruction via distributed instruction by proposing innovations such as the use of an index of average learning outcomes as a measure of educational output or the derivation of an average costs function that includes measures of learning productivity and faculty and staff productivity. Jewett's nine basic propositions help to form a mind-set for higher education that addresses the IT challenges for distributed learning.

The chapter by Jones and Jewett lists a number of steps and provides a table to guide planners who are considering the development and delivery of courses through the Internet, CD-ROM, and interactive video technologies. The "costing activity structure" includes course activities, academic support, student services, and institutional support. An additional table titled "Prototype Cost Assignment Summary" will help administrators evaluate costs such as operating expenditures (e.g., compensation for faculty, curriculum planning, paraprofessional support), capital costs, supplies, and additional expenses.

The chapter by Klaudis and Stine approaches the topic of expanding costs for IT by presenting basic and unavoidable principles to apply for cost management. The authors propose a paradigm that administrators can follow in attempting to manage costs (e.g., the infrastructure or utility level, institutional management practices, and policy level), strategic investment, and the lower level, where institutional planning and strategy take place.

Landry's chapter describes the notion of ubiquitous computing (making computers available to students and faculty alike) as a means of developing the use of technology in teaching and learning. The author proposes the idea of leasing rather than buying such equipment for a campus technology "backbone." Landry lists the benefits of shifting the IT budget from capitol to operating budgets and shares the lessons other institutions have learned.

Leach and Smallen's chapter reports on longitudinal data gained about higher education institutions from a collaborative project called "COSTS." By studying these data and becoming participants in the study, planners can prepare a realistic IT budget for their own institutions that include certain benchmarks such as the dollar amount spent per student.

The chapter by Maitland, Hendrikson, and Dubeck examines issues affecting faculty compensation and costs brought about by information technology. Surprisingly, a number of findings from their research suggest that in-person instruction may always be less expensive than instruction via the Internet. The authors discuss how the use of lower-paid personnel rather than regular faculty to cut costs can affect the quality of instruction.

The chapter by Pumerantz and Frances offers a wide-angle view and a way to estimate and track an institution's expenses as it moves into newer information technology ventures. The authors also discuss some of the trade-offs to students and faculty that their research reveals. They provide questions to guide administrators and policy makers when making IT decisions about expanding access, enhancing quality, and cutting costs.

On the topic of assessment, Caplan's chapter reports on his research challenging the notion that no significant differences exist in educational outcomes between classroom-based and technology-mediated learning for distance learning students. He offers a set of questions for researchers to consider in their own assessment of student satisfaction.

BUDGET AND FUNDING

◀ Orivel, François. **Finance, Costs and Economics**. In *Basic Education at a Distance: World Review of Distance Education and Open Learning*, vol. 2, ed. Chris Yates and Jo Bradley, 138–52. New York: Routledge/Farmer, 2000. ISBN 0415237734.

Orivel discusses the development of the ideas of a world system of education and universal access to a basic education—a feat still unattainable for poorer, undeveloped countries. He compares the cost of teaching via computer and suggests to planners that it is cheaper and more likely to succeed with the implementation of new information and communication technologies.

FACULTY ISSUES

◀ **Being There Is What Matters**. *Academe* 85, no. 5 (September/October 1999): 32–36.

This special issue of *Academe* focuses on distance education and its perceived threats to higher education. These threats include displacing the live, personal interaction necessary for learning; loss of educational quality; a professor's intellectual property rights; reduction of the size of faculty as online programs replace traditional ones; a professor's loss of control of the curriculum; and a widening gap between private and public liberal arts colleges. These issues are vital concerns for administrators and educators alike.

◀ Bower, Beverly L. **Distance Education: Facing the Faculty Challenge.** *Online Journal of Distance Learning Administration* IV, no. 11 (Summer 2001). (26 pars). http://www.westga.edu/~distance/ojdla /summer42/bower42.html (26 March 2002).

Bower succinctly reviews the concerns (such as institutional support, promotion and tenure, workload, and training) of faculty who are expected to teach on the Internet. Campus administrators must reckon with these changes and those occurring in the interpersonal relationships with their students and with the issue of the quality of instruction.

◀ Gilcher, Kay W., and Margaret A. Chambers. **Web Initiative in Teaching: A Strategy of Faculty Leadership Development and Institutional Capacity Building.** Paper presented at the Annual Conference on Distance Teaching and Learning '99, University of Wisconsin-Madison, August 1999. ERIC, ED 440287.

Gilcher and Chambers describe an excellent Fellows program titled Web Initiative in Teaching (WIT), a model for faculty development crucial to institutions entering the distance learning environment. The Fellows and Web instructional designers worked in teams to develop course modules. Valuable practices that emerged from the project include the development of criteria for peer evaluation of courses and peer review for mentoring and assessment of teaching, a focus on student outcomes for Web-based learning, and institutional procedures and policies needed to support distance learning. Institutional commitment and financial support for the workshops, Fellows' expenses, release time, and/or overload are of primary importance to any Web curriculum initiative.

◀ Noble, David F. **Technology and the Commodification of Higher Education.** *Monthly Review* 53 (10): 26–40. March 2002. (32 pars.). Online. *ProQuest.* (23 March 2002).

This article is based on David Noble's book, *Digital Diploma Mills: The Automation of Higher Education* published by Monthly Review Press in 2002. Noble critically examines the push for distance education as the commodification or commoditization of higher education and its campaign for profit. This is done at the expense of the goals and values of education (developing self-knowledge), abandoning the student-teacher relationship, and initiating the deprofessionalization of faculty. Noble criticizes the growth of online education as a commodity or commercial transaction that alienates the people involved in the educational process by forcing them to surrender their ownership of course materials to the production of materials for sale.

Noble takes the reader through the development of for-profit online institutions such as Jones University and examines how major trade associations such as the American Council of Education and others who once fought against the accreditation of these institutions, now are competing for the same market, which, in reality, may not exist. What is notable about this article and Noble's book are the recent developments including the effects of the dot-com collapse and its impact on online education cutbacks and the intrusion of the government (i.e., Department of Defense), now partnering with higher education institutions to become a broker and consumer of distance learning in the United States, bringing with it far-reaching consequences for those institutions. Offering a glimmer of hope for safeguarding higher education goals, Noble reports on the movement among professional associations and college and university systems to fight back.

◀ White, Frank. **Digital Diploma Mills: A Dissenting Voice**. *First Monday* 4 (1999). http://www.firstmonday.dk/issues/issue4_7/white/ (27 March 2002).

In this essay White addresses the concern that Web-based technology promotes social control over faculty and students. A major concern discussed is faculty members' intellectual rights. However, White also supports distributed learning technologies. This issue reflects the debate experience in academic circles that is of great importance to both faculty and the institution for which they work.

TECHNOLOGY

◀ Aggarwal, Anil, ed. **Web-Based Learning and Teaching Technologies: Opportunities and Challenges**. Hershey, PA: Idea Group, 2000. ISBN 1878289608.

This book is a compilation of individually authored chapters by practitioners from a number of countries including France, Finland, Australia, Sri Lanka, and China. Each author describes his or her Web-based teaching and learning experiences. The value of this book for administrators and practitioners is that it reflects on the experiences of others—what has worked or not worked and the possibilities and pitfalls of Web-based learning, while also assessing where and how to use it for their own institutions or teaching and learning experiences.

The book is divided into four sections. The authors in the first section present an overview of Web-based learning from kindergarten through the university level and discuss the need to develop an infrastructure for developing countries. Web-based learning services, tools, software, and pedagogy are reviewed in the second section. The third section reviews such topics as the management of course assignments, assessment techniques, and faculty development. The final section provides a number of Web-based learning research studies from the United States and abroad.

◀ Anderson, Terry. **Interaction Options for Learning in the Virtual Classroom.** Academic Technologies for Learning. http://www.atl .ualberta.ca/articles/disted/interact_options.cfm (27 March 2002).

Anderson describes the role of "interactivity" (or the nature of the communication that takes place) and its importance in the learning community for producing meaning and understanding. The author looks at how this learning takes place among students in the virtual classroom. Anderson compares asynchronous interaction (e.g., e-mail, listservs, newsgroups, computer conferencing) and synchronous communication (e.g., Internet voice telephone, videoconferencing, text-based chats, text-based virtual learning environments, graphical virtual reality environments, and Net-based virtual lecture room systems). The author provides a list of learning activities for the virtual classroom, such as debates, brainstorming, panel discussions, suggestions on how to use interactivity effectively, and a list of resources for its facilitation.

◀ Asirvatham, Sandy. **Beyond the Distance Barrier.** *Journal of Property Management* 65, no. 5 (2000): 42–48.

This thoughtful article reviews the role of various forms of distance learning that involve synchronous learning. The author points out that videoconferencing can be very expensive (from $100 to $7,000 for software and from $150 to nearly $5,000 for hardware) and requires a great deal of bandwidth. A virtual conference system can cost around $158,000. It is still much cheaper to use synchronous telephone conference calls to communicate and remain interactive. The author states that the graphics and technological bells and whistles of a Web class will be ineffective if students aren't continually encouraged to think for themselves, solve problems, and seek instant feedback. This article reinforces the notion that, even in distance learning, the focus needs to be on the students' learning of new skills.

◀ Bates, A. W. **Managing Technological Change Strategies for College and University Leaders.** San Francisco: Jossey-Bass, 2000. ISBN 0787946812.

The author—an experienced writer, researcher, and technologist—writes for decision makers, administrators, other technologists, and faculty on the topic of the impact of new technologies on educational systems. In this book he covers a gamut of issues dealing with technology, including developing the infrastructure, planning and managing courses and programs, supporting faculty, costs, funding strategies, collaborative efforts, competition, and reviewing the research. Lists of tables provide information on the costs of classroom teaching, computer conferencing, and funding.

◀ Belanger, France, and David H. Jordon. **Evaluation and Implementation for Distance Learning: Technologies, Tools, Techniques.** Hershey, PA: Idea Group, 2000. ISBN 1878289632.

Belanger and Jordan provide an overview of distance learning in higher education and industry, especially in the areas of implementing and evaluating programs using Web-based training (WBT), teleconferencing using audio and video, video teletraining (VTT), and computer-aided instruction (CBT). This book describes many of the issues in online education, and includes such topics as course development and instructional design. The authors describe distance learning technologies and tools, their use, and their advantages and disadvantages for researchers and practitioners.

◀ Chute, Alan G., Pamela K. Sayers, and Richard P. Gardner. **Networked Learning Environments.** http://www.lucent.com/cedl/networked-learning.htm (April 2000).

These authors suggest that instructors and education providers need to harness the potential of asynchronous and synchronous communication technologies in order to create powerful, learner-centered networks and a mosaic of networked learning environments reflective of the educational provider's mission, the learners' expectations, and the instructors' delivery style. They give examples of this networking capability and describe the role of the instructor in a learning network; the role of the support services infrastructure, which provides resources for the student; ways to provide virtual library resources (e.g., integrated voice, video, and data resources) to the distant learner; and a virtual learning environment. They also address the issues of delivery and preservation of a session and the future of the networked learning environment.

◀ Conway, Eugenia D., Thomas E. Cyrs, and John P. Skonk. **Instructional Technology Decisions: Designed for Learning or WWWWWWW (Whew!): Why We Went With the World Wide Web.** Paper presented at the Annual Conference on Distance Teaching and Learning '99, University of Wisconsin-Madison, August 1999. ERIC, ED 440287.

A number of technologies are available for delivering distance learning courses. How can an institution select the ones that are the most appropriate for its needs? The authors of this paper describe a graduate-level course for students with teaching experience. Using a six-step model that analyzes traditional courses, they help identify which technologies are appropriate to use for each course. The authors also discuss learning outcomes.

◀ Distance Learning in Higher Education. **The Expanding Universe of Distance Learning**. The Institute for Higher Education Policy for the Council for Higher Education Accreditation, February 1999. http://www.ihep.com/Pubs/PDF/ace.pdf (24 March 2002).

This report provides an update to the issues and information resulting from a campus computing survey conducted in 1998, which studied the use of technology in higher education and the issues facing colleges and universities today (e.g., helping faculty integrate technology into instruction, providing adequate user support, and financial planning for the information technology). The report provides statistics on the use of e-mail, the percentage of classes using Internet resources, the explosion of high-speed networks, and the ways in which institutions are dealing with matters such as student fees for technology and policies for intellectual property.

◀ Franklin, Nancy, and Donald E. Kaufman. **Transforming Faculty for Distance Learning**. Paper presented at the Annual Conference on Distance Teaching and Learning '99, University of Wisconsin-Madison, August 1999. ERIC, ED 440287.

Indiana State University instituted an approach to prepare faculty for the distance education environment by establishing the Course Transformation Academy (CTA) faculty development program. Faculty trained at CTA to design courses for the Web. A focus was placed on three areas: instructional design utilizing effective strategies (e.g., discussion threads, chat rooms, video and audioconferencing, instructional videos, multimedia software, etc.); pedagogy for sound teaching principles; and the proper selection of media technology. This university not only took advantage of the distance learning technologies to serve the needs of its students throughout the state in obtaining a four-year degree, but also provided the necessary training for its faculty at the same time.

◀ Gladieuz, Lawrence E., and Scott Swail. **The Virtual University and Educational Opportunity: Issues of Equity and Access for the Next Generation**. Washington, D.C.: College Board, 1999. OCLC 42320553.

This report discusses the global impact of information technology on distance education and examines the issue of access specifically for those who are not yet able to participate in this new educational technology. The authors discuss training requirements and the need for policy change, and they ask probing questions such as: Who will regulate a global market? Will the new technologies save or add to educational costs? Excellent appendixes include global information on Websites listing courseware or distance learning information, professional associations, and both for-profit and non-profit companies.

◀ **Guidelines for Good Practice: Effective Instructor-Student Contact in Distance Learning.** The Academic Senate for the California Community Colleges. http://www.academicsenate.cc.ca.us /Academic%20Senate%20Web/Publications/Papers/good_practice _distance.html (26 March 2002).

These guidelines, adopted by the Academic Senate for California Community Colleges in the spring of 1999, address good practices of all types of technology-mediated instruction, whether on campus or through distance learning. Curriculum guidelines spell out requisites for developing a curriculum model and for adherence to distance education curriculum review requirements for educators and administrators. The "Effective Contract for Distance Learning" lists guidelines for various types of distance learning modes of instruction (e.g., video, multimedia, or Web-based instruction). Collective bargaining issues are also included (e.g., class size). Most helpful are the appendices, which provide a variety of forms, questions, answers, and so on that a course proposer or local curriculum committee could use.

◀ Hardin, Joseph, and John Ziebarth. **Digital Technology and Its Impact on Education.** 12 January 2000. National Center for Supercomputing Applications. http://www.ed.gov/Technology/Futures /hardin.html (26 March 2002).

Hardin and Zieberth review the impact of digital technology over the last two decades and focus their attention on the collaborative technology of the Internet and communication issues concerning higher education. The authors look at the benefits of asynchronous communication vehicles (e.g., e-mail, bulletin boards, newsgroups, and listservs) and synchronous communication vehicles (e.g., desktop videoconferencing, chat sessions, Multi-User Dungeons (MUDs), Object-Oriented MUDs (MOOs), or Multi-User Shared Hallucinations (MUSHes). They describe various types of software and focus on developing a Web infrastructure that would provide capabilities directly targeted at globally distributed research and learning communities. The authors strongly suggest that colleges and universities collaborate and become leaders in applying these technologies to education.

◀ Kolloff, Mary Ann, Fred Kolloff, and Joyce Thomas. **Instructional Design Models and Distance Education.** Paper presented at the Annual Conference on Distance Teaching and Learning '99, University of Wisconsin-Madison, August 1999. ERIC, ED 440287.

The authors review instructional design models and tasks, institutional considerations, and faculty concerns such as time constraints, an analysis of the learner, delivery of content, and selection of technology. This paper is more theoretical in nature and focuses on the philosophy of faculty, educational philosophy, learner outcomes, and instructional strategies. All are necessary considerations for designing instruction for the Web.

◀ Meachen, Ed., and Hal Schlais. **The University of Wisconsin Distributed Learning System.** Paper presented at the Annual Conference on Distance Teaching and Learning '99, University of Wisconsin-Madison, August 1999. ERIC, ED 440287.

Meachen and Schlais describe the evolution of a distributed learning system (DLS) at the University of Wisconsin's 26 campuses. SONET, the statewide communications backbone, includes a wide-area ATM (asynchronous transfer mode) network and the wiring of all UW campuses allowing teachers and students to interact virtually anywhere. The authors describe the Web-based tools, faculty and program development support structures (e.g., resource sharing among faculty and institutions), and program and course delivery (e.g., online delivery of two extended-degree programs, a criminal justice degree program, a nursing degree program, an arts degree program, and a global hospitality and tourism Master's degree program).

◀ Milliron, Mark David, and Cindy L. Miles, eds. **Taking a Big Picture Look at Technology, Learning, and the Community College.** Mission Viejo, CA: League for Innovation in the Community College, 2000. ISBN 0615111521.

This book is a valuable resource for administrators, technology planners, policy makers, faculty, and staff. It presents a number of perspectives on the ways in which technology is affecting teaching and learning; the growth of distance learning, cyber-counseling and virtual registration, and student services in the information age; marketing through technology; and transformation issues for community colleges, such as ways to unleash the power of the Internet for higher education. The chapters provide a comprehensive look at how technology has brought about not only many changes, issues, and challenges, but also opportunities for growth.

◀ Ndahi, Hassan B. **Utilization of Distance Learning Technology Among Industrial and Technical Teacher Education Faculty.** In *Journal of Industrial Teacher Education* 36, no. 4 (1999). http://scholar.lib.vt.edu/ejournals/JITE/v36n4/ndahi.html (26 March 2002).

Ndahi reports the results of a study that examines the extent to which distance learning technology is used by faculty in industrial and technological teacher education programs. He reviews how faculty members react to using distance learning technologies and whether their attitudes toward using technologies such as satellite delivery, television broadcasts, compressed video, computer conferencing, multimedia, audioconferencing, radio, and videotapes influence how effectively they are used for instruction and how they contribute to improved teaching and learning. The article suggests that administrators should target younger faculty members for professional development, consider workload adjustments, and provide training, support, resources, and encouragement.

◀ Pilkington, Rachel M., and Catherine L. Bennett. **Evaluating CHAT Seminars Within a WebCT Networked Learning Environment**. Paper presented at Networked Learning 2000: Innovative Approaches to Lifelong Learning and Higher Education Through the Internet, International Conference, Lancaster, England, 17–19 April 2000. ERIC, ED 441078.

Pilkington and Bennett report on the use of a virtual learning environment (VLE) developed to provide learning support for potential distant students. The VLE used WebCT, computer-mediated communications, and Web tools located by icons for CHAT, a bulletin board, and course content. A detailed report on the study analyzes the positive and negative experiences using CHAT. This information will be important for administrators, faculty members, or instructors.

◀ Saunders, Gary, and Rick Weible. **Electronic Courses: Old Wine in New Bottles?** *Internet Research: Electronic Networking Applications and Policy* 9, no. 5 (1999): 339.

The authors report on a survey assessing attitudes and perceptions of accounting chairpersons who use electronic courses. Almost 65 percent of the respondents viewed electronic courses or the teaching of students online as negative. They perceived the courses as being similar to the correspondence courses of the past, only using new technology. They also observed that student-to-instructor and student-to-student interactions were missing. Although electronic courses continue to grow, the respondents' concerns are with the relevance of the traditional college or university. Will these become a relic of the past? The survey's results indicate the need for more study by administrators.

PARTNERSHIPS

◀ Carliner, Saul. **Administering Distance Courses Taught in Partnership with Other Institutions**. *Online Journal of Distance Learning Administration* IV, no. 11 (Summer 2001). http://www.westga.edu /~distance/ojdla/summer42/carliner42.html (26 March 2002).

Carliner identifies 13 administrative issues that arise for faculty who teach distance education courses to students enrolled in other institutions. Administrators and faculty need to consider these matters to ensure that students will be successful distant learners. The author describes the administrative models for institutions that are forming this type of partnership and discusses the role of an institution's culture, registration, scheduling, academic calendars, support services, grading, technology, and relationships with its students.

◀ Levy, Jonathon D. **Convergence: Strange Footprints to Virtual Universities.** Paper at the Annual Conference on Distance Teaching and Learning '99, University of Wisconsin-Madison, August 1999. ERIC, ED 440287.

Higher education leaders may wish to consider opportunities for global learning if they are to compete in today's educational arena. In this paper, the author comments on a new hybrid of education characterized by a convergence of media, program platforms, delivery modalities, and pedagogies. Levy describes various models of collaboration between businesses and higher education that have sprung up in this new environment. The new technologies allow both synchronous and asynchronous communication to take place and thus open up possibilities of greater collaboration between businesses and academia for continued education worldwide.

◀ Stallings, Dees. **Perspectives On ... Pros and Cons of Partnering: A VCampus Perspective.** *Journal of Academic Librarianship* 27, no. 1 (Jan. 2001): 52. EBSCOhost Academic Elite (Accession no. 4112966).

The author examines the advantages and disadvantages of developing online partnerships among various academic institutions and Vcampus—a company that focuses on technology, pedagogy, and marketing. Stallings reviews Vcampus services and addresses issues such as ownership of the courses, provision of technical support, infrastructure, and training for instructors and course developers. Universities have the great task of developing and providing the infrastructure, training, and services. This type of partnership is crucial to a university's success in meeting its goals for providing distance learning. This article helps institutions to determine whether this type of partnership might be beneficial to them.

ACCREDITATION AND REGULATIONS

There is no single authority responsible for postsecondary educational institutions in the United States. Accreditation for postsecondary institutions arose with the merging of two bodies—the Federation of Regional Accrediting Commissions of Higher Education and the National Commission on Accrediting—and became the Council of Postsecondary Accreditation (COPA) in 1974.[11] Regional and national private educational associations came together to conduct nongovernmental, peer evaluation of educational institutions and programs. They developed criteria for institutional or program evaluation along with a set of accrediting procedures. The basic procedures include: (1) the development of standards, (2) a self-study or in-depth self-evaluation by the institution or program, (3) on-site evaluation by a team from the accrediting agency, (4) listing in an official publication of the institution's status, and (5) a periodic reevaluation.[12]

A current list of regional accrediting agencies recognized by the U.S. Secretary of Education is accessible from the Office of Postsecondary Education.[13] The National Advisory Committee on Institutional Quality and Integrity reviews each agency periodically to establish eligibility to participate in Title IV programs. A list of these agencies with a brief description of each is posted on the Web.[14] In addition, a number of national institutional and specialized accrediting bodies categorized by discipline (e.g., allied health, business, Christian education, clinical laboratory science, etc.) can also be found on the Web.[15] A distance education and training Website provides up-to-date information about the accreditation process for distance learning.[16] There is a link on this site to a list of accredited higher education distance learning institutions with degree programs.

◄ **Higher Education 2000: What Will Be New? What Will Be Different?** Proceedings of AQA '99, 1999. Philadelphia: Middle States Commission on Higher Education, 2000. OCLC 48711472.

This book is a collection of essays written for the 1999 Annual Accreditation and Quality Assurance Conference sponsored by the Commission on Higher Education of the Middle States Association of Colleges and Schools. The theme of the conference reflects the changing landscape of higher education as it is influenced by distance learning and addresses the issue of accreditation as it relates to institutions both in the United States and abroad. The essays cover topics such as college, corporate, and community partnerships; emerging issues in the expansion of continuing education programs; accountability and assessment; international education; collaboration among colleges; and successful partnerships between public schools and community colleges. Of importance to administrators is the concluding chapter, "The Review of Characteristics of Excellence in Higher Education: Standards for Accreditation," which lists a number of guiding principles or standards for the review process for colleges and universities.

Another chapter of interest in *Higher Education 2000* is the one by Cambridge, Hamilton, and Kahn. These authors discuss the Urban Universities Portfolio Project which developed electronic institutional portfolios for six urban, public universities. The portfolios are a showcase of examples of student work, with assessment and critiques showing the outcomes, processes, and practices the students used to achieve those results. Given its visibility on the Internet, the project's goal is to reflect its mission, its research and scholarship, and its accomplishments in student learning to the community, students, parents, stakeholders (e.g., the students' employers, the Higher Education Commission, taxpayers, legislators, etc.), and external stakeholders (e.g., accrediting agencies, other higher education institutions, and future faculty). Given this visibility on the Web, the opportunity arises for any college or university to create electronic portfolios for evaluation of its own mission, practices, and accomplishments.

Readers will also be interested in the chapter by Sir John Daniel, titled "Medium and Message: Passion, Values, and Quality in the New Academy." Daniel discusses accreditation and quality as it relates to the United States Open University (USOU) and the Open University of the United Kingdom, which itself is an accreditation body. The author talks about the beginnings in 1969 of the Open University, known as the world's most successful distributed teaching university, and its unchanged mission: "Open as to people, open as to places, open as to methods, and open as to ideas."[17] This has also been adopted by the United States Open University with the addition of "Open as to time and open to the world."[18] Daniel includes a review of each discipline's curriculum design, content, and organization; teaching, learning, and assessment; student progress and achievement; student support and guidance; learning resources; and quality assurance and enhancement.[19] He stresses the importance of preserving the notion of a community of scholars interested in teaching and research. If quality and value are to be characteristics of distance learning programs, then these two influences are critical considerations.

CHALLENGES

◀ Altbach, Philip G. **The Crisis in Multinational Higher Education.** *Change* 32, no. 6 (November/December 2000): 28–31. Proquest database.

Altbach focuses on the challenges and problems that arise from the growth of technology and international collaboration by asking administrators and all involved to stand back and analyze the new realities of multinational distance education. For example, the author mentions a number of important factors, such as the financial motive for establishing multinational distance learning programs; the fact that institutions operate in an unregulated environment; and the observation that institutions such as Jones International and the University of Phoenix are not real universities, but rather degree-delivery machines that provide tailored programs for specific markets and therefore should not be called universities. This article cautions institutions planning to get into the multinational market to consider this information carefully.

◀ Cini, Marie A., and Boris Vilic. **Online Teaching: Moving from Risk to Challenge.** *Syllabus* 12, no. 10: 38–40, 1999.

Cini and Vilic inform administrators of the technological issues of an online Web environment and the needs of faculty. The authors discuss faculty fears about teaching online (e.g., educational quality, the replacement of faculty by computers, cheating issues, course ownership, and misperceptions of what constitutes an online course). They recommend that administrators offer an online minicourse designed for faculty to help them overcome technophobic attitudes and other anxieties, to encourage them to engage in online ventures, to discuss these questions within the university community, and to provide incentives (e.g., credit toward tenure, release time, and monetary incentives). Administrators who help faculty make this transition comfortably will, in the long run, ensure the highest quality of teaching and learning online.

◀ Green, Joshua. **The Online Education Bubble**. *The American Prospect* 11, no. 22 (23 October 2000): 32–35. Proquest (August 2001).

Green outlines one of the challenges faced by institutions of higher education—that is, the competing of for-profit virtual universities (e.g., the University of Phoenix, Jones University, or Capella University) for the nontraditional online student market. The author warns that online education could be the latest overhyped Internet concept in which the supply overestimates the demand and that even prestigious institutions such as Stanford, Harvard, and Duke should be aware that money—not pedagogy—is behind these partnerships. Green points out the dangers to institutions, such as the excessive costs for course development, lack of student support services, and problems with marketing.

◀ **The Internet, Distance Learning and the Future of the Research University**. Hearing Before the Subcommittee on Basic Research of the House of Representatives One Hundred Sixth Congress. 9 May 2000. Serial no. 1-6-81. Washington, D.C.: U.S. Government Printing Office.

A Congressional hearing reviews distance learning experiences for higher education institutions through the testimony of those in the field. Among those testifying are experts from the American Association of Universities, the Center for Advanced Educational Services, WebCT, and the University of Michigan. The hearing offers an excellent view of distance learning projects and is a valuable report of others' experiences.

◀ Kohn, Kay J., and Jules LaPidus. **Post-Baccalaureate Futures: New Markets, Resources, and Credentials**. Westport, CT: Greenwood, 2000. ISBN 1573563609.

This book is intended to guide higher education administrators and policy makers as they try to meet the demand for postbaccalaureate learning. The authors examine tough issues such as competition from the private sector, the influence of new technologies on teaching and learning for faculty and students, and the need for revenue and accreditation.

◀ Stallings, Dees. **The Virtual University: Organizing to Survive in the 21st Century**. *Journal of Academic Librarianship* 27, no. 1 (January 2001): 12. EBSCOhost Academic Elite (Accession no. 4112950).

Stallings looks at the ways in which we have already become "virtual institutions" through the medium of the Internet (e.g., e-mail, e-commerce for global shopping, common global libraries or universities). He lists questions that institutions should be asking themselves about distance learning regardless of predictions that computers will surpass human intelligence and affect the way we learn. The author predicts that humans—not computers—will be the dominant presence both online and on campus. This lengthy and informative article reviews the influences of the fragmented distance learning market, the role of the government, accreditation commissions, profit or nonprofit alliances, and the challenges for the virtual university of the future. Stallings makes several recommendations for institutions as they prepare to meet the future and the growth of the virtual university.

◀ Van Dusen, Gerald C. **Digital Dilemma: Issues of Access, Cost, and Quality in Media-Enhanced and Distance Education.** New York: Jossey-Bass, 2000. ISBN 0787955736.

Van Dusen examines the potential and perils of the digital age with regard to philosophical issues concerning the purposes of education. Universal access, age, income, race, gender, physical or learning disabilities, and affordability, as well as the issues of quality and effectiveness are topics he covers for everyone concerned, especially for institutions eager for change. His list of recommendations strives for equality and a high-quality education for all.

ASSESSMENT

◀ Calder, Judith, and Santosh Panda. **Evaluation and Quality.** In *Basic Education at a Distance: World Review of Distance Education and Open Learning*, vol. 2, ed. Chris Yates and Jo Bradley, 110–21. New York: Routledge/Farmer, 2000. ISBN 0415237734.

These authors stress the importance of accountability to the stakeholders of distance learning programs and identify various evaluation approaches. They give the advantages and disadvantages of each.

◀ Robertson, Mitchell J. **Successful Student Assessment Strategies.** Paper presented at the Annual Conference on Distance Teaching and Learning '99, University of Wisconsin-Madison, August 1999. ERIC, ED 440287.

Web-based courses offer a challenge to student assessment. The topics Robertson addresses in this paper include the evaluation of student progress in a course for assigning fair grades in a Web-based course and ways to encourage and ensure academic honesty for assignments, exercises, or exams. The author proposes a number of valuable strategies faculty can use for a valid assessment of students in nontraditional courses. Robertson lists important points for Web course instructors from *Effective Grading: A Tool for Learning and Assessment.*[20] He also gives practice examples of courses and student assessment methods used for each course based on the assignments for that particular course. This paper gives practical advice on assessment and offers a model that is helpful to instructors.

◀ Yates, Chris. **Outcomes: What Have We Learned?** In *Basic Education at a Distance: World Review of Distance Education and Open Learning*, vol. 2, ed. Chris Yates and Jo Bradley, 229–45. New York: Routledge/Farmer, 2000. ISBN 0415237734.

Yates summarizes outcomes for open and distance education with regard to policy, access, costs, equity, quality, and effectiveness. The author provides tables that list distance learning models or projects in several countries, information about each, and their costs in terms of U.S. dollars.

◀ Yates, Chris, and Jo Bradley, eds. **Basic Education at a Distance: World Review of Distance Education and Open Learning**, vol. 2. New York: Routledge/Farmer, 2000. ISBN 0415237734.

This volume reviews case studies of distance and open learning ventures worldwide for a number of settings. The authors examine successful and not-so-successful distance learning initiatives that will be of interest to educators, administrators, education planners, policy makers, and lending and development agencies.

COPYRIGHT/FAIR USE

Distance education courses now on the Web are highly visible, making it easier for copyright infringements to take place. Various media formats can be combined with new materials, preexisting materials, and live lectures, thus causing confusion over specific rights. It is also possible to have a wide variety of intellectual property owners involved in a course. Rights must be acquired to use materials, as well to transmit the course over various types of networks. What about future uses of the course for distribution, transmission, and taping? All of these factors must be considered before the course is delivered. The following section reviews the literature on distance education copyright issues.

◀ **AAUP Special Committee on Distance Education and Intellectual Property Issues.** May/June 1999. Archived at http://www.aaup.org /lduc/bibliog.htm (23 March 2002).

The American Association of University Professors (AAUP) established a Special Committee on Distance Education and Intellectual Property Issues in 1998. The areas of focus were faculty compensation, intellectual property rights, and academic freedom. Two policy statements, "Statement of Distance Education" and "Statement on Copyright," can be found on the AAUP Website. The committee developed two documents, "Suggestions and Guidelines: Sample Language for Institutions' Policies and Contract Language on Distance Education" and "Suggestions and Guidelines: Sample Language for Institutional Policies and Contract Language on Ownership of Intellectual Property." The sample language was taken from existing policies, contracts, and AAUP policy statements. This site is of importance to faculty who need to be aware of their rights and restrictions in developing curriculum and course materials. The site will also help administrators to understand where they stand legally in these discussions.

◄ Colyer, Anita. **Copyright Law, the Internet, and Distance Education**. In *Web-Based Communications, The Internet, and Distance Education*, ed. Michael Moore and Geoffrey T. Cozine, 109–20. University Park, PA: The American Center for the Study of Distance Education, 2000. ISBN 1877780243.

Colyer discusses issues related to copyrights for online course development and delivery that are important for and helpful to online course providers. The author provides a short history of copyright law, ways in which new technologies are shaping interpretations of the law, and recent lawsuits and case studies.

◄ **Copyright in the New Millennium: The Impact of Recent Changes to U.S. Copyright Law.** A Satellite Teleconference cosponsored by the American Association of Law Libraries, American Library Association, Association of College and Research Libraries, Medical Library Association, and the Special Libraries Association. Washington, D.C.: George Washington University Library. 21 May 1999. http://nnlm.gov/psr/lat/v8n3/copyright.html (23 March 2002).

In 1998 the 105th Congress passed two bills to amend the 1976 Copyright Act: (1) the Digital Millennium Copyright Act (DMCA), intended to update copyright law for the digital age in selected arenas and (2) the Sonny Bono Copyright Term Extension Act, which gives copyright owners another 20 years of copyright protection for their works. Significantly, a third piece of legislation, database protection, did not pass in 2000 and has been reintroduced in the House this session. The current bill has the potential for fundamentally changing the way the research and education community works.

These changes to copyright law enacted by the 105th Congress have significant implications for libraries, archives, and institutions of higher education. Of particular importance are the portions of the DMCA that contain detailed regulations that online service providers must follow to obtain liability protection for infringement. Not only must online service providers register with the Copyright Office, but educational institutions are also required to educate their communities about copyright law and compliance. Other sections of the law require the community to develop long-term protection of fair use and other copyright exceptions. In addition, changes to the law are still possible, as Congress directed the Copyright Office to study ways to use digital technology to promote distance education. This document also provides an overview of the new laws involving copyrights and the key issues in complying with these. The new act makes numerous changes in U.S. copyright law.

◀ Crews, Kenneth D. **Fair Use: Overview and Meaning for Higher Education.** http://www.iupui/~copyinfo/highered2000.html (24 March 2002).

Crews describes what constitutes fair use of a copyrighted work, including reproductions, comments, news reporting, teaching (including multiple copies for classroom use), scholarship, or research. Four factors are described from the fair-use statute: purpose, nature, amount, and effect. Several cases that offer guidance for colleges and universities are included on this Website.

◀ **The Digital Millennium Copyright Act.** Archived at http://www.educause .edu/issues/dmca.html (17 April 2002).

This EDUCAUSE Current Issues Web page provides access to the Digital Millennium Copyright Act, the most comprehensive reform of the United States copyright law that now includes an update for the U.S. copyright law for the digital age in preparation for ratification of the World Intellectual Property Organization (WIPO) treaties. The topics reviewed in the DMCA provisions include fair use in a digital environment and online service provider (OSP) liability. This EDUCAUSE site also provides links to additional documents such as: (1) the *U.S. Copyright Office Summary of the Digital Millennium Copyright Act of 1998*, legislation appearing in Acrobat format (http://lcweb.loc.gov/copyright/legislation/dmca.pdf) (17 April 2002); (2) the *Copyright Office Conducts Study on How to Promote Distance Education Through Digital Technologies*, a study conducted by the Copyright Office with representatives of copyright owners and nonprofit educational institutions and libraries (http://www.educause.edu/issues/digitaltech.html) (17 April 2002); (3) the *EDUCAUSE Statement on Copyright Office Interim Regulations for Service Providers*, a letter for members that explains the interim regulations for the Digital Millennium Copyright Act and recommends a course of action by which universities can take advantage of the protections offered to those who are also service providers (http://www.educause.edu /netatedu/contents/reports/agentletter981110r.html) (17 April 2002); and (4) *Highlights of New Copyright Provision Establishing Limitation of Liability for Online Service Providers*, a memorandum that explains the new DMCA provisions pertaining to OSP liability, including "notice-and-takedown" requirements, "notice and put-back," and certain safe harbors contained in Title II of the Digital Millennium Copyright Act.

◀ Diotalevi, Robert. **Copyright in Cyberspace: Practices and Procedures in Higher Education.** *Syllabus* 12, no. 9 (1999): 51–52.

Many American colleges and universities are addressing copyright law by publishing their policies, some via the Internet. Diotalevi reports that two courses, titled "Copyright Law" and "The Law of Cyberspace," are included in the College of West Virginia's curriculum. The college instituted copyright policies for the Internet, e-mail, and issues related to software, media services, usage/transmissions, passwords, and privacy. The author provides a list of resources for institutions to use as a model for creating a copyright policy such as the United States Copyright Office (http://www.lcweb.loc.gov /copyright/) (17 April 2002) and the Copyright Clearance Center's Guidelines for Creating a Policy for Copyright Compliance (http://www.copyright.com) (17 April 2002). The guidelines include a statement of corporate values; sources of U.S. copyright law; a statement of corporate obligations regarding copyright; an outline of compliance procedures; and instructions for handling an incident of copyright infringement. Diotalevi refers to a comprehensive model for education that was created by the University of Georgia's State Copyright Regents Committee, "The Regents Guide to Understanding Copyright and Educational Fair Use" (http://www.peachnet.edu/admin/legal/copyright /copy.html) (25 March 2002). The author makes a number of helpful suggestions for colleges or universities that are developing their own policies and includes a list of universities that have their policies posted online.

◀ Gasaway, Laura N. **Distance Learning and Copyright: Is a Solution in Sight?** In *CAUSE/EFFECT* 22, no. 3 (1999). http://www.educause .edu/ir/library/html/cem9932.html (17 April 2002).

Gasaway reviews the issues raised by the new copyright law and the obstacles that have arisen in institutions and faculties. The author looks at the classroom exemption that does not have the broad exception it once had before the new Digital Millennium Copyright Act. For example, distance courses cannot transmit musical works without getting permission from the copyright holder and paying royalties. This paper discusses the fair use exemption and its implications for distance learning. Gasaway reviews the history of the amending of the Copyright Act and the opposition raised by the Association of American Publishers and Viacom. This is a debate that is certainly not over. It is important to follow the course of the debate, issues, and problems brought about by the new law and to ensure compliance.

◀ Hochman, Michael C. **Beware What You Ask For**. *Intellectual Property Magazine* (11 June 1999).

Hochman reviews the arguments for and against government regulation of the Internet. The author discusses Congress's reluctance to respond to demands for regulation and suggests that Congress may try to police other aspects of the Internet (e.g., the provision of Internet service) and thus begin a new round of legal challenges. The communication industry is growing rapidly through the development of new high-speed service by cable providers, wireless providers, broadcast stations, and telephone providers in delivering broadband services to consumers. Competition by companies such as AT&T and US West and partnerships between America Online (AOL) and Bell add to the growing environment for developing delivery systems and for addressing problems in the future. It is important for those in higher education to follow these issues and the implications for their institutions.

◀ Lide, Casey. **What Colleges and Universities Need to Know About the Digital Millennium Copyright Act**. In *CAUSE/EFFECT Journal* 22, no. 1 (1999). http://www.educause.edu/ir/library/html/cem9913 .html (17 March 2002).

The Digital Millennium Copyright Act contains provisions that affect college and university administrators, faculty, and students. This essay focuses on two of the DMCA's provisions. The first is the limitation on infringement liability for service providers who are defined as "a provider of online services or network access, or the operator of facilities therefore."[21] Lide describes four categories that limit liability of the service provider. They are: (1) transitory digital network communications, (2) systems catching, (3) information location tools, and (4) information on systems or networks at the direction of users. The second provision concerns the circumvention of technological protection measures (TPMs). This section covers two types of technical measures to protect copyrighted works—those that prevent unauthorized access to and those that prevent unauthorized copying of a copyrighted work.[22] The author suggests that colleges and universities take advantage of the opportunity to limit their liability as online service providers by registering with the Copyright Office as an agent to receive notification of claims of copyright infringement. In order to understand the ramifications of the Digital Millennium Copyright Act, colleges and universities need to educate their campus communities on the copyright law and enlist the services of their legal counselors. The author provides a quick checklist for campus actions to guide colleges and universities in this process.

◄ Lipinski, Thomas. **An Argument for the Application of Copyright Law to Distance Education.** In *Web-Based Communications, The Internet, and Distance Education*, ed. Michael Moore and Geoffrey T. Cozine, 51–61. University Park, PA: The American Center for the Study of Distance Education, 2000. ISBN 1877780243.

Lipinski focuses on the copyright issues most pertinent to distant education, Web-based instruction, and the construction of electronic reserves (also called virtual libraries). He examines both the dangers of moving toward the compulsory licensing of information products and services and ideas on fair use legislation.

◄ Luker, Mark. **Copyright Office Conducts Study on How to Promote Distance Education Through Digital Technologies.** In *EDUCAUSE Current Issues* (28 April, 1999). Archived at http://www.educause.edu/issues/digitaltech.html (26 March 2002).

In this paper EDUCAUSE discusses its participation in the Copyright Office's study on how to promote distance learning through digital technologies, while maintaining an appropriate balance between the rights of the copyright owners and the needs of users of copyrighted works. In March 1999 EDUCAUSE stated a number of concerns in its reply, for example, changes were needed in the copyright law if intellectual property licensing practices are to flourish in the digital arena. EDUCAUSE also stated that as content providers, colleges and universities have a vested interest in protecting the market value of copyrighted work and that current licensing methods are not sufficient for allowing students to use the works for educational purposes. EDUCAUSE compiled a list of exemptions—guiding principles for the use of copyrighted works for higher education.

◄ Milone, Michael. **Digital Millennium Act Revises Copyright Legislation; Government Activity.** *Technology and Learning* 6, no. 19 (1999): 60.

Milone describes how the Digital Millennium Copyright Act preserves the fair use of copyright for libraries and educational institutions through the use of technology (e.g., computer programs). He provides examples of what constitutes "fair use," what is considered a violation of fair use and the copyright law, and who becomes liable in the case of alleged infringement—the student or the institution.

◄ **Report on Copyright and Digital Distance Education: A Report of the Register of Copyrights.** Vols. 1–3. Washington, D.C.: U.S. Copyright Office, 1999. ISBN 0160500672.

This report provides an extensive overview of copyright issues involved in digital distance education. It discusses the nature of distance education today and describes current licensing practices in digital education, including problems and future trends. It also describes the status of the technologies already available or in development relating to the delivery of distance education courses and the protection of their content. The report also discusses prior initiatives to address copyright issues through the negotiation of guidelines or the enactment of legislation. Volume 1 provides the Congressional mandate and the Copyright Office process; an overview of distance education today; the evolution of asynchronous and synchronous technologies; providers, partnerships, and federal legislation;[23] and the licensing of copyrighted works.[24] Volume 1 also includes sections on digital distance education technologies,[25] the application of the Copyright Law and prior initiatives addressing copyright and digital distance education,[26] and recommendations for amending the current Copyright Act.[27] Appendixes include the "Marketplace for Licensing in Digital Distance Education," which examines the role of licensing in digital distance education; "Fair Use Guidelines for Educational Multimedia"; and "Proposal for Educational Fair Use Guidelines for Distance Learning."

Volume 2 contains the comments of more than 50 colleges, universities, associations, and organizations that participated in the public hearings. This volume contains the recommendations for amending the Copyright Law. An example of one of the comments comes from the working group and copyright committee of the Indiana Commission for Higher Education (ICHE) and the Indiana Partnership for Statewide Education (IPSE), who participated in revising the Copyright Law to "promote distance education through digital technologies." An agreement reached by representatives from 22 colleges and universities in Indiana details the scope of distance education today and the problems confronting educators in applying existing section 110(2) of the copyright law to distance education initiatives. This group proposes solutions that could enhance students' educational opportunities and still maintain the economic and intellectual integrity of authors' works. A statement of principles defines the nature of distance education, the role of licensing, the use of technology, and the application of the Copyright Law to distance education. Similar recommendations come from the American Society of Composers, Authors, and Publishers; Elsevier Science Publishers; Prentice Hall Publishers; the National Music Publishers' Association; and many others.

Volume 3 contains a wealth of information and views taken from the experiences of organizations, colleges, and universities. These include the ways in which key associations, organizations, and institutions of higher education deal with important copyright issues. Examples of these are the Global Distance Learning Association;[28] the universities of Maryland, Delaware, and Nebraska;[29] the American Association of University Professors;[30] the Motion Picture Association of America; Time Warner, Inc.;[31] the Association of Research Libraries; the American Library Association; the American Association of Law Libraries; the Special Libraries Association; and the Medical Library Association.[32]

◀ **Reproduction of Copyrighted Works by Educators and Librarians.**
Washington, D.C.: United States Copyright Office. http://www.loc.gov
/copyright. Available in PDF format at http://www.loc.gov/copyright
/circs/circ21.pdf (26 March 2002).

This booklet covers the subject of fair use and photocopying provisions of the Copyright Law and the major concerns of professors, librarians, and archivists in the reproduction (for the purposes of study, research, interlibrary exchanges, and archival preservation) of copyrighted materials for students. Materials include books, periodicals, and music. Although this booklet does not specify the distribution of copyrighted materials to students via the Web, it provides the background law on exclusive rights in copyrighted works and fair use. The booklet includes excerpts from the House, Senate, and conference reports. Information on photocopying multiple copies, systematic reproduction, interlibrary loan arrangements, and guidelines for off-air recording of broadcast programming for educational purposes can be found in the discussion.

◀ Sanoff, Alvin. P. **Whose Property Is It Anyway?** *ASEE Prism* 9, no. 9 (May/June 2000): 18–22.

Sanoff reviews the question of intellectual property rights for work that a professor creates. Examples of questions at the center of the debate in academia are the following: Does an institution have a right to share in the revenue from a course designed by a faculty member but distributed outside its walls by others? Does a professor have a right to contract with an outside entity for dissemination of a course without the institution's prior approval? If the professor's university, rather than an outside firm, distributes the course, is the professor entitled to a share of the "profits," and, if so, what is an appropriate percentage? And who owns the course anyway—the professor or the university? Sanoff provides an example of such a case at Harvard, where a professor created a Web course on civil procedure that was distributed online by another university. Harvard's concerns (and the concerns of other universities) are that this changes the relationship between the professor and the university; that this creates an opening for for-profit corporations to offer large amounts of money to the Harvard faculty to teach online, thus diminishing the value of Harvard courses to traditional students; and that there exists the possibility of misusing a university's name online. Sanoff reviews for administrators and faculty how some universities such as Cornell, Princeton, and the Georgia Institute of Technology are responding to these problems.

◀ **Welcome to fairuuse.stanford.edu. Copyright and Fair Use.**
http://fairuse.stanford.edu/ (18 March 2002).

This Stanford University Libraries' Web page provides access to articles and documents related to copyright and fair use. The Website is a wonderful source of information for colleges and universities. It includes links to primary materials such as statutes, judicial opinions, regulations, treaties, and conventions. Another area of research covers current legislation, cases, issues (e.g., fair use and multimedia information), National Information Infrastructure (NII) legislation, the Michigan Document Services (MDS) case, and coursepacks (the MDS appeal was not heard by the U.S. Supreme Court). In addition, links are provided to Websites and mailing lists, library copyright guidelines, articles on copyright and fair use; the WIPO Database Proposal and HR 3531; the copyright Website from Benedict O'Mahoney, Timeline: A History of Copyright in the U.S.; U.S. Supreme Court cases since 1893, and U.S. Constitution annotated links to U.S. Supreme Court cases.

In conclusion, the preceding sources are probably the most important for administrators of institutions to reflect on. We hope that the literature we have reviewed provides a solid overview of the issues and concerns for institutions. A study of the literature and the experiences of other higher education institutions will be inevitable as distance education continues to evolve and bring with it still more benefits and concerns.

NOTES

1.   Advertising Your Distance Learning Program. In *Creating the Virtual Classroom Distance Learning with the Internet,* by Lynnette R. Porter, 173–89. New York: John Wiley, 1997. ISBN 0471178306.

2.   Stallings, Dees. Perspectives On . . . Pros and Cons of Partnering: A Vcampus Perspective. *Journal of Academic Librarianship* 27, no. 1 (January 2001): 52 EBSCOhost Academic Elite (Accession no. 4112966).

3.   Stallings, Perspectives On…Pros and Cons of Partnering, 1.

4.   Covington, Richard. Students Log On for Virtual Education—Internet Learning Programs Emerging as E-Commerce's New Frontier. *International Herald Tribune* 23 (June 2000).

5.   Stallings, Perspectives On…Pros and Cons of Partnering, 1.

6.   Daniel, J. S., *Mega-Universities and Knowledge Media: Technology Strategies for Higher Education,* 4–55. London: Kogan Page, 1996.

7.   Goldberg, Edward D., and David M. Seldin. The Future of Higher Education in an Internet World Twilight or Dawn? In *Dollars, Distance, and Online Education: The New Economics of College Teaching and Learning,* ed. Martin J. Finkelstein, Carol Frances, Frank I. Jewett, and Bernhard W. Scholz, 297. Phoenix: The Oryx Press, 2000. ISBN 1573563951.

8. MacDonald, Gerard. Universities and Knowledge Economies: A Paradigmatic Change? Unpublished paper, Networked Learning 2000: Innovative Approaches to Lifelong Learning and Higher Education Through the Internet, April 2000. Sheffield University. ERIC, ED 441078.

9. Castells, Manuel. *Critical Education in the New Information Age.* Lanham, Maryland: Rowman and Littlefield, 1999.

10. MacDonald, 2000.

11. Accreditation in the United States, available from the World Wide Web at http://www.ed.gov/offices/OPE/accreditation/accredus.html (26 March 2002).

12. Ibid.

13. Nationally Recognized Accrediting Agencies, available from the World Wide Web at http://www.ed.gov/offices/OPE/accreditation/natlagencies .html (26 March 2002).

14. Ibid.

15. National Institutional and Specialized Accrediting Bodies, available from the World Wide Web at http://www.ed.gov/offices/OPE/accreditation/natlinstandspec.html (7 August 2001).

16. The Distance Education and Training Council, available from the World Wide Web at http://www.detc.org/ (7 August 2001).

17. Daniel, Sir John. Medium and Message: Passion, Values, and Quality in the New Academy. In *Higher Education 2000: What Will Be New? What Will Be Different? Proceedings of AQA '99,* 1999. (Philadelphia: Middle States Commission on Higher Education, 2000): 18.

18. Ibid., 19.

19. Ibid., 20.

20. Walvoord, Barbara E., and Virginia Johnson Anderson. *Effective Grading: A Tool for Learning and Assessment.* San Francisco: Jossey-Bass, 1995. ISBN 6787940305.

21. *The Digital Millennium Copyright Act of 1998,* U.S. Copyright Office Summary (December 1998). [s. 512(k)(1)(A)]. Available on the World Wide Web at http://lcweb.loc.gov/copyright/legislation/dmca.pdf (17 March 2002).

22.   Ibid. [Section 1201].

23.   *Report on Copyright and Digital Distance Education: A Report of the Register of Copyrights.* Vol. 1, 9–27. Washington, D.C.: U.S. Copyright Office, 1999. ISBN: 0160500672.

24.   Ibid., 29–46.

25.   Ibid., 49–67.

26.   Ibid., 69–125.

27.   Ibid., 127–69.

28.   Ibid., Vol. 3, 10–19.

29.   Ibid., 78–98.

30.   Ibid., 138–51.

31.   Ibid., 195–208.

32.   Ibid., 277–84.

Teaching and Learning Community

As the number of distance learning programs continues to grow, the need for additional research on the impact of these programs on faculty and students also grows. For faculty members, distance learning courses require additional time, training, and technical support. The faculty members are also faced with several unanswered questions—ones that need to be explored further: (1) Who owns and controls the intellectual property in a course produced for distance learning? (2) How do the different modes of transmission affect the use of materials in a distance learning context? (3) How can distance learning be used to maximize students' learning experiences? and (4) How can the faculty's traditional role in determining academic and pedagogical issues ensure that maximization?[1]

Who are the students who enroll in distance education courses? The average distance learning student is a highly motivated mature adult who often has difficulty balancing academic responsibilities with his or her personal life and work life. Although much of the current research reports student satisfaction with distance learning courses, one of the complaints most often heard is about the lack of interaction with classmates and the instructor. "While asynchronous modes of presentation allow for anytime, anywhere" education, the distance learning student loses the dynamism of real-time teacher-student and student-student interaction.[2]

These are some of the problems facing faculty and students in distance learning programs. The following sections explore these and related issues.

FACULTY

◄ **Distance Education: Guidelines for Good Practice.** American Federation of Teachers, 2000. Online. FirstSearch. http://www.aft.org /higher_ed/downloadable/distance.pdf. (18 April 2002).

Based in part on the responses to a survey the American Federation of Teachers (AFT) conducted of AFT members who use distance education, this report presents a set of guidelines for good practice in distance education. A summary of the survey, plus selected individual responses, appears at the end of the report.

◄ Hereford, Lady. **NEA Poll Delves into Distance Learning.** *Community College Week* 12, no. 24 (2000): 30. EBSCOhost. (3 March 2001).

This report presents the results of a poll conducted by the National Education Association concerning its U.S. members' views on distance education in higher education.

◄ Inman, Elliot, Michael Kerwin, and Larry Mayers. **Instructor and Student Attitudes Toward Distance Learning.** *Community College Journal of Research and Practice* 23 (1999): 581–91.

Eleven community college instructors and the 334 students enrolled in their distance learning classes were surveyed as to their attitudes toward distance learning. Results of the study are discussed.

◄ Lamb, Annette, and William L. Smith. **Ten Facts of Life for Distance Learning Courses.** *TechTrends* 44, no. 1 (2000): 12–15. Online. FirstSearch. Education Abs. Article number BEDI00013527. (22 August 2001).

The authors provide 10 perceptive tips that review teaching strategies readers may already know but may not have thought to incorporate into their distance learning courses.

◄ Schifter, Catherine C. **Faculty Motivators and Inhibitors for Participation in Distance Education.** *Education Technology* (2000): 43–46.

This report presents the results of a survey distributed to full-time faculty, deans, and administrators at an urban Research 1, state-related institution to determine how they view faculty participation in distance education.

◄ Visser, James A. **Faculty Work in Developing and Teaching Web-Based Distance Courses: A Case Study of Time and Effort.** *The American Journal of Distance Education* 14, no. 3 (2000): 21–31.

This article presents the results of a study that explored whether distance education courses require greater work effort and time obligations than traditionally taught courses. Implications for future research and faculty participation are discussed.

TRAINING

◄ Tedd, Lucy, Milena Tetrevova, and Clare Thomas. **Training Librarians in the Production of Distance Training Materials: Experiences of the PROLIB Project.** *Education for Information* 18, no. 1 (2000): 67–76.

The authors provide background on the Professional Development Programme for Slovak Librarians (PROLIB) and focus on a "training the trainers" workshop. This article may be useful in planning, running, and evaluating a training workshop that will not be in the participants' native language and where participants have varying levels of knowledge or experience in educational practice and information and communications technologies.

◄ Wells, Richard C. **Back to the (Internet) Classroom.** *Training* 36, no. 3 (Minneapolis 1999): 50–52. Online. FirstSearch. WilsonSelect_FT. Article number BBPI99021584. (3 March 2001).

This article explores how a small training company came to the conclusion that distance learning using the Internet was for them. Factors to consider are discussed.

STUDENTS

◄ Baillie, Caroline, and Gilda Percoco. **A Study of Present Use and Usefulness of Computer-Based Learning at a Technical University.** *European Journal of Engineering Education* 25, no. 1 (2000): 33–43. Online. Proquest. 14 March 2001.

"It is important to identify optimum conditions for the use of information and communication technologies (ICT) to give the best results in a specific educational environment" (33). This article reports the results of a study of the problems, advantages, disadvantages, and effectiveness of computer-assisted learning (CAL)/ICT.

◀ Christensen, Edward A., Uzoamaka P. Anakwe, and Eric H. Kessler. **Receptivity to Distance Learning: The Effect of Technology, Reputation, Constraints and Learning Preferences.** *Journal of Research on Computing in Education* 33, no. 3 (2001): 263–79. Online. FirstSearch. EducationAbs. Article number BEDI015770. (22 August 2001).

The authors view distance learning from the student's perspective before experiencing distance learning (i.e., a priori attitudes and preferences), focusing on student receptivity toward the medium.

◀ Dede, Chris. **The Multiple-Media Difference.** *TECHNOS* 8, no. 1 (1999): 16–18.

The author describes his graduate course on learning across distance that uses seven instructional media. Four of the interactive media are synchronous (e.g., face-to-face interaction, videoconferencing, synchronous interactions in a text-based virtual world called Tapped In [www.tappedin.sri.com], and "Groupware," which incorporates a shared design space). Two others are asynchronous (asynchronous threaded discussions and asynchronous telementoring). The seventh medium (Websites structured around an ongoing interaction or experience) is both synchronous and asynchronous.

◀ Farmington, Gregory, and Stephen C. Bronack. **Sink or Swim?** *T.H.E. Journal* 28, no. 10 (2001): 70–76. Online. FirstSearch. EducationAbs. Article number BEDI0105743. (22 August 2001).

Farmington and Bronack present "The Clipper Project," which is a unique and valuable multiyear initiative designed to investigate the short- and long-term effects of online classes.

◀ Gallagher, Peggy Ahrenhold, and Katherine McCormick. **Student Satisfaction with Two-Way Interactive Distance Learning for Delivery of Early Childhood Special Education Coursework.** *Journal of Special Education Technology* 14, no. 1 (1999): 32–47 (50 pars.). Online. FirstSearch. *WilsonSelect_FT.* Article number BEDI99018101. (6 December 2000).

The focus of this article is on distance learning research in four specific areas (the attitude/satisfaction of students regarding the delivery of coursework, student/faculty interaction during the delivery of coursework, student outcomes in distance education coursework, and faculty satisfaction with delivery and coursework). The article discusses these areas in the context of using two-way interactive television (ITV) to deliver distance education to college students.

◀ Hilgenberg, Cheryl, and William Tolone. **Student Perceptions of Satisfaction and Opportunities for Critical Thinking in Distance Education by Interactive Video.** *The American Journal of Distance Education* 14, no. 3 (2000): 59–73.

A number of general studies measure student satisfaction with distance learning, but Hilgenberg and Tolone have narrowed their research to focus on distance learning and the use of critical thinking.

◀ Petracchi, Helen E. **Distance Education: What Do Our Students Tell Us?** *Research on Social Work Practice* 10, no. 3 (2000): 362–76. Online. Proquest. (27 March 2001).

Literature that addresses remote students' perceptions of their learning experience is limited, and Petracchi's discerning article helps to fill that gap. Students were enrolled at two urban campuses where their classes either used interactive television (ITV) or pre-recorded videotapes.

◀ Phillips, Melodie R., and Mary Jane Peters. **Targeting Rural Students with Distance Learning Courses: A Comparative Study of Determinant Attributes and Satisfaction Levels.** *Journal of Education for Business* 74, no. 6 (1999): 351–56. Online. *WilsonSelect Plus_FT*. Article number BEDI99024027. (9 March 2001).

Nontraditional and off-campus students have needs, wants, and expectations that differ from those of traditional students. This study investigates urban/suburban vs. rural distance learning students' needs.

◀ Sankaran, Siva R., Dalila Sankaran, and Tung X. Biu. **Effect of Student Attitude to Course Format on Learning Performance: An Empirical Study in Web vs. Lecture Instruction.** *Journal of Instructional Psychology* 27, no. 1 (2000): 66-72 (26 pars.). Online. FirstSearch. *WilsonSelect_FT*. Article number BEDI00013886. (6 December 2000).

This is an informative article that examines how students differ in their choice of Web and lecture formats. Additionally, the authors investigated how student attitudes toward these two course formats affected their learning performance, the relationship between attitude to course format and the students' learning strategy, and the differences in attitudes toward the Web format among various ethnic groups and ESL students.

◀ Small, Ruth V. **A Comparison of the Resident and Distance Learning Experience in Library and Information Science Graduate Education.** *Journal of Education for Library and Information Science* 40 (1999): 27–47.

In 1993 Syracuse University's School of Information Studies began a distance education program for part-time students, known as the MLS Independent Study Degree Program (MLS-ISDP). The author conducted her research on the experiences of both the resident students (those who commute to the campus) and distance education students by using three main data-gathering techniques: a questionnaire, focus group sessions, and interviews.

◀ Sonner, Brenda S. **Success in the Capstone Business Course: Assessing the Effectiveness of Distance Learning.** *Journal of Education for Business* 74, no. 4 (1999): 243–47.

This study examines student success in the final Capstone business class after having taken one or more distance learning courses. The three distance learning options the students could choose from included classes via television, a "learning contract" (under the direction of an assigned faculty member the student completes required coursework independently), and college level examination program (CLEP) credit.

◀ Spooner, Fred, Luann Jordon, Bob Algozzine, and Melba Spooner. **Student Ratings of Instruction in Distance Learning and On-Campus Classes.** *Journal of Educational Research* 92, no. 3 (1999): 132–40.

This study compares opinions of a course that was offered both on and off campus in different semesters and also compares student ratings of distance learning courses offered at local and off-campus facilities.

◀ Stainfield, John, Peter Fisher, Bob Ford, and Michael Solemn. **International Virtual Field Trips: A New Direction?** *Journal of Geography in Higher Education* 24, no. 1 (2000): 255–62.

This article briefly traces the development of Virtual Field Trips (VFTs), discusses their advantages and disadvantages, and includes a short list of existing VFT materials accessible via the Internet. Although "we are many years away from creating a VFT that could be properly called virtual reality where the user is fully immersed in an interactive computer-generated environment," this article will serve as a good introduction to VFTs (260).

◀ Terrell, Steven R., and Laurie Dringus. **An Investigation of the Effect of Learning Style on Student Success in an Online Learning Environment.** *Journal of Education Technology Systems* 28, no. 3 (1999–2000): 231–38.

Although the results of their study are not statistically significant, Terrell and Dringus made some interesting discoveries. On a cautionary note, although most students can succeed in an online learning environment regardless of their learning style, institutions that offer Internet-based distance education programs should be aware that students have different learning styles. These institutions thus need to be prepared to address learning style issues when they are developing, utilizing, and marketing these programs.

NOTES

1.   Distance Learning. *Academe* 84, no. 3 (1998): 30–38.

2.   Ravaglia, Raymond, and Richard Sommer. Expanding the Curriculum with Distance Learning. *Principal* 79, no. 3 (2000): 10–13 (24 pars.). Online. FirstSearch. *WilsonSelect_FT*. Article number BEDI99035517. (6 December 2000).

Distance
Learning
Programs

"With increasing numbers of adult learners and the need for more afford-able education choices, demands for educational opportunities have called for the creation of more convenient times and locations."[1] "The attraction of a new revenue stream coupled with the fear of being left behind is driving colleges and universities online in droves. Today, 75 percent of two- and four-year colleges offer some form of online education."[2] By 2001 that number will reach 90 percent, with online programs competing for many of the 100 million Americans expected to take part in continuing education by 2004.[3] Unfortunately, many colleges and universities are investing heavily in online education without totally understanding the "extent of what is required to create, market and maintain a viable online program that will hold up to competition."[4]

But is there a down side to distance education? Do distance learning classes remove the human interaction that some students still require? Issues such as the design and production of courseware, objectives, competencies, and learning outcomes (OCLs), and the use and implications of critical think-ing, various technologies (e-mail, television, interactive video), as well as questions of the dehumanization of the classroom, the replacement of whole programs with online substitutes, the faculty's loss of control of the curricu-lum, and the quality and comparability of distance learning and instruction with traditional methods continue to be important topics that demand further research.

CURRICULUM

◄ Green, Joshua. **The Online Education Bubble.** *The American Prospect* 11, no. 22 (2000): 32–35. Online. Proquest. (27 March 2001).

Green makes several thought-provoking statements in his article. He addresses the questions of whether sufficient demand exists, who will survive this rapidly changing field of distance education, and whether those schools that aren't ready will be left behind. "If the supply of online education outweighs the demand, conditions are ripe for a shakeout" (32). This is a must-read for colleges and universities considering a totally online education program.

◄ Martin, W. Allen. **Being There Is What Matters.** *Academe* 85, no. 5 (1999): 32–36.

Although Martin is definitely in the minority when he states that distance learning poses a number of threats to higher education, despite administrators' hopes that it will help them to outdo the competition, he makes credible arguments to support his theories (i.e., distance education is a threat to educational quality and professors' intellectual property). This compelling article is definitely food for thought.

◄ Navarro, Peter, and Judy Shoemaker. **Policy Issues in the Teaching of Economics in Cyberspace: Research Design, Course Design, and Research Results.** *Contemporary Economic Policy* 18, no. 3 (2000): 359–66. Online. Proquest. (27 March 2001).

In this article the authors examine issues in course and research design. Although their focus is on cybereconomics, their research results will prove useful to those institutions seeking to implement any curriculum in a rigorous and pedagogically sound manner.

◄ Reeve, Derek, Susan Hardwick, Karen Kemp, and Teresa Ploszajska. **Delivering Geographic Courses Internationally.** *Journal of Geography in Higher Education* 24, no. 2 (2000): 228–37. Online. Proquest. (14 March 2001).

With their focus on the pedagogic, institutional, and business requirements of international distance learning rather than the technological requirements, these authors discuss their varied experiences. Their observations will be beneficial to anyone currently contemplating the development of an international distance learning program.

EVALUATION

◀ Boling, Nancy C., and Daniel H. Robinson. **Individual Study, Interactive Multimedia, or Cooperative Learning: Which Activity Best Supplements Lecture-Based Distance Education?** *Journal of Educational Psychology* 91, no. 1 (1999): 169–74.

This study investigated whether students would benefit from the addition of either a cooperative learning or an interactive media activity following a distance learning lecture. Results of the postlecture activity study show that when measuring for learning, cooperative learning is better than either individual study or interactive media. However, when looking at student satisfaction ratings, interactive media comes out ahead of cooperative learning and individual study. Further research is recommended, specifically looking at more effective ways of combining cooperative learning and interactive media.

◀ Clow, Kenneth E. **Interactive Distance Learning: Impact on Student Course Evaluations.** *Journal of Marketing Education* 21, no. 2 (1999): 97–105.

Clow compares the impact of interactive distance learning to the traditional classroom approach at both graduate and undergraduate levels. Discussion of this perceptive study includes practical steps that one can take to correct the problems the negative evaluations point out.

◀ Diaz, David P., and Ryan B. Cartnal. **Students' Learning Styles in Two Classes: Online Distance Learning and Equivalent On-Campus.** *College Teaching* 47, no. 4 (1999): 130–35.

This article explores the results of a study that compares the learning styles of distance learning students with those of traditional students enrolled in identical health education courses.

The assessment tool the authors chose was the Grasha-Reichmann Student Learning Style Scales (GRSLSS). Results indicate that students in distance learning and off-campus courses exhibit different learning styles. Independent students who favor self-paced instruction chose online courses. Students who prefer more structure and less independent instruction chose the traditional, on-campus courses.

The authors discuss suggested uses for social learning style inventories and their results. They include suggestions for designing class delivery meth ods and choosing educational technologies.

◀ Kubala, Tom. **Teaching Community College Faculty Members on the Internet.** *Community College Journal of Research and Practice* 24, no. 5 (June 2000): 331–40.

Kubala describes his experiences at the University of Central Florida in designing and teaching Web-based graduate courses (part of a doctoral program) to faculty members in community colleges. These courses are "The Community College in America" and "The Community College Curriculum." Kubala includes tips on designing course materials and enlisting the aid of technical experts. Kubala refers to his "11 canons for distance learners." These same canons (e.g., do your homework, be an explorer, help each other and your instructor, have a life besides this course) would be useful to all students taking courses through the Web. The faculty members completed their course evaluations electronically. Evaluation of the course drew positive feedback from the faculty-students, who said they would consider Web-based teaching for their own students.

◀ Leasure, A. Renee, Lisa Davis, and Susan L. Thievon. **Comparison of Student Outcomes and Preferences in a Traditional vs. World Wide-Based Baccalaureate Nursing Research Course.** *Journal of Nursing Education* 39, no. 4 (2000): 149–54 (48 pars.). Online. FirstSearch. *WilsonSelect_FT*. Article number BEDI00012708. (1 January 2001).

The purpose of this project is twofold: first, to compare undergraduate student outcomes for a course that was conducted using both the World Wide Web (WWW) and traditional methods; second, to discover the reasons students chose either a Web-based or a traditionally taught class. Results indicate no significant differences in student test scores or course grades. Reasons for choosing a Web-based course include cost, flexibility, and convenience. Those who chose the traditional course style valued interaction with classmates and felt they would be less likely to succumb to procrastination.

◀ Merisotis, Jamie P., and Ronald A. Phipps. **What's the Difference? Outcomes of Distance vs. Traditional Classroom-Based Learning.** *Change* 31, no. 3 (1999): 12–17 (33 pars.). Online. FirstSearch. *WilsonSelect_FT*. Article number BEDI99016825. (6 December 2000).

What's the difference between distance learning and traditional classroom-based instruction? Merisotis and Phipps take a closer look at the issue of distance learning's effectiveness and focus their research on an original report that included experimental, descriptive, correlational, and case studies. Their conclusions are divided into four groups: (1) the research findings; (2) key shortcomings of the research; (3) gaps in the research; and (4) implications.

◄ Schulman, Allan H., and Randi L. Sims. **Learning in an Online Format Versus and In-Class Format: An Experimental Study.** *Technological Horizons in Education (T.H.E.) Journal* 26, no. 11 (1999): 54–56.

Schulman and Sims provide the results of a study comparing the effectiveness of online learning to that of a traditional class. The authors affirm the advantages of online teaching (e.g., its easy accessibility, as well as its cost when compared to traditional education). The authors cite similar studies that show that students who studied online did statistically better than traditional in-class students (e.g., the University of Phoenix students scored 5 to 10 percent higher, and Cal State Northridge students scored an average of 20 percent higher). They conclude that their own findings cannot be generalized because of the limited number of students enrolled and that additional research is necessary to test the effectiveness of online instruction.

◄ Urken, Arnold B. **Taking Assessment Online.** *ASEE Prism* 9, no. 2 (1999): 29–30 (13 pars.). Online. FirstSearch. *WilsonSelect_FT*. Article number BEDI99027903. (6 December 2000).

Urken asserts that although there are advantages to using Web-based surveys, researchers should exercise caution. Though such surveys are easy to create and administer, they may not produce high-quality results. Urken also discusses four issues to consider when designing a Web-based survey: (1) don't automatically adopt a sampling approach; (2) make surveys part of a learning process; (3) don't become obsessed with response rates; and (4) examine the implications of using different scoring mechanisms.

◄ Warf, Barney, Peter Vincent, and Darren Purcell. **International Collaborative Learning on the World Wide Web.** *Journal of Geography* 98, no. 3 (1999): 141–48 (40 pars.). Online. FirstSearch. *WilsonSelect_FT*. Article Number BEDI99039340. (6 December 2000).

This article examines the design, implementation, and results of a unique project. The project was originated by faculty in geography and educational research at Lancaster University, United Kingdom, and expanded to include five faculty members and 16 student volunteers from three institutions: Lancaster University; University College, Galway, Ireland; and Florida State University, Tallahassee. The goal of the project was "to investigate the potential of long-distance, collaborative, student learning on an international basis" (142).

Two of the problems the students encountered were technical glitches and the lack of time to browse the Web and find and evaluate suitable sites. Despite these problems, the project verifies that long-distance collaboration through cyberspace is possible and should be considered a form of fieldwork—virtual fieldwork.

NOTES

1.   Boling, Nancy C., and Daniel H. Robinson. Individual Study, Interactive Multimedia, or Cooperative Learning: Which Activity Best Supplements Lecture-Based Distance Education? *Journal of Educational Psychology* 91, no. 1 (1999): 169–74.

2.   Green, Joshua. The Online Education Bubble. *The American Prospect* 22, no. 22 (2000): 32–35.

3.   Ibid.

4.   Ibid.

Role of the Library

Due to the increase in the number of available instructional technologies, an expectation has arisen that library services will be accessible to students in remote locations. Students' expectations include 24-hour access to user-friendly online databases, 24-hour help desk support, instruction, contact information for requesting assistance, interlibrary loan request information, and rapid response time for requested materials, reference requests, and informational questions.[1] To meet these needs, librarians are moving away from traditional lecture modes of instruction and exploring ways in which they can facilitate, rather than direct, students' learning to locate and use information.[2] They are forming new partnerships with campus faculty and overcoming the limitations of collections and distance by scanning material into a networked electronic reserve system, thereby improving access to the quantity and range of materials, as well as the number and distribution of learners.[3]

It is imperative that librarians take a proactive stance so that libraries can be a part of the rigorous planning and development efforts that distance learning entails. "If training workshops for distance education faculty are offered, the distance education librarian should be a presenter at this training. As distance offerings are listed each term the distance education librarian should make contact, informing faculty of the types of services available and opening discussions about the students' library needs for success in the course."[4] The inclusion of library staff in distance learning programs increases the visibility of the library and its programs to the library's community of users. "It also influences their perception and expectations about the library and staff. As new models of distance learning continue to be developed and implemented, the roles library staff undertake will need to continue to change and evolve, yet the central purpose remains the same—helping students to learn to use the library resources and services effectively."[5]

SUPPORT SERVICES

◀ Ault, Meredith, and Rachel Viggiano. **Going the Distance: Traditional Reference Services for Non-Traditional Users.** *Florida Libraries* 43, no. 2 (2000): 6–7. Online. *WilsonSelectPlus_FT.* Article number BLIB00017906. (11 March 2001).

This informative article discusses the Florida Distance Learning Reference and Referral Center's (RRC) mission to provide library research support to distance learning students. The RRC also assists distance learning faculty by providing them with in-class, online, or broadcast instruction sessions for their students. These sessions teach the students ways to conduct library research from a distance, access individualized class Web pages that link to course-related research materials, and print materials that outline the available library resources and services. In addition, the sessions discuss how the librarians are involved in designing and marketing their services.

◀ Cervone, Frank, and Doris Brown. **Transforming Library Services to Support Distance Learning: Strategies Used by DePaul University Libraries.** *College and Research Libraries News* 62, no. 2 (2001): 147–49.

Keeping the fundamental mission of most academic libraries in mind ("to promote, assist, and provide access to information services for the entire campus community"), the authors make important recommendations to ensure that the needs of distance learning students will be met. The three major areas they target are: (1) ways to expand digital collections, (2) physical access and delivery, and (3) ways to design the Website for patrons.

◀ Cutler, Kay A., Beth Blanton-Kent, and Judy Jordan. **Going the Distance: Instructional and Reference Services in Distance Learning.** *Virginia Libraries* 45, no. 1 (1999): 6–8.

Discussion focuses on three models (one-to-many instruction, case method of instruction, and collaborative instruction) of distance learning and the library support provided for each.

◀ Davis, Hazel M. **Distance Learning Students and Library Services: Issues, Solutions, and the Rio Salado College Model.** *Community and Junior College Libraries* 9, no. 2 (2000): 3–13.

Although some institutions still face the restructuring of their traditional campus systems to support distance courses, Rio Salado College (AZ) modified its support systems to support a nontraditional infrastructure more than 20 years ago. Davis outlines Rio Salado's model for library services.

◀ Hufford, Jon R. **The University Library's Role in Planning a Successful Distance Learning Program.** *Reference Librarian* 69 (2000): 193–203. Copublished simultaneously as *Reference Services for the Adult Learner: Challenging Issues for the Traditional and Technological Era*, ed. Kwasi Sarkodie-Mensah, 193–203. Binghamton, NY: Haworth Press, 2000.

Hufford looks at the role a university library should play in planning student support services (reference, information literacy instruction, document delivery services) using Texas Tech University's Distance Learning Council's efforts to plan, prioritize, and develop a distance learning program to illustrate what is vital to the success of a distance learning program.

◀ Hughes, Carol Ann, Ilene Rockman, and Lizabeth A. Wilson. **Communicating Resource Needs for Successful Library Services.** *Bottom Line* 13, no. 1 (2000): 10–15.

This article focuses on library budgets and suggests ways to increase the budget for both library services and programs. The authors also list the five best budget practices.

◀ Jenkins, Christine. **Far Out Learning.** *School Library Journal* 46, no. 2 (2000): 46–49.

Skeptical that an online class could effectively create a "community of learners," Jenkins discovered that, by using the right technology, a virtual class would feel as real as a traditional class. The author's distance learning classroom experiences will be of particular help to youth services and school librarians.

◀ Kirk, Elizabeth E., and Andrea M Bartelstein. **Libraries Close in on Distance Education.** *Library Journal* 124, no. 6 (1999): 40–42. Online. Proquest. (14 March 2001).

Out of necessity, librarians and information professionals are learning both to adapt and promote their services for distance education. Using examples from various colleges and universities, the authors show how libraries are getting involved in planning and promoting their role in distance learning.

◀ Maxymuk, John. **Internet: Distant Learning.** *Bottom Line* 13, no. 1 (2000): 45–50.

The Association of College and Research Libraries' (ACRL) Guidelines for Distance Learning Library Services (July 1998) are discussed, emphasizing that "Members of the distance learning community are entitled to library services and resources equivalent to those provided for students and faculty in traditional campus settings" (46–47). The author discusses the extent to which the University of Phoenix, Old Dominion University (VA), New York University, and Western Governors University are acting in accordance with these guidelines.

◀ Meola, Marc, and Sam Stormont. **Real-Time Reference Service for the Remote User: From the Telephone and Electronic Mail to Internet Chat, Instant Messaging, and Collaborative Software.** *Reference Librarian* 67/68 (1999): 29–40.

This article presents an edifying comparison of the more established technologies for reaching remote users (the telephone and electronic mail) with emerging technologies (Internet chat, instant messaging, and collaborative software). The authors also highlight Temple University's efforts to reach remote users in real time with an interactive pager program called TalkBack.

◀ Ryer, Mary Ann, and Birte Nebeker. **Implementing an "Ask a Librarian" Electronic Service.** *Community and Junior College Libraries* 9, no. 1 (1999): 21–34.

These authors discuss the thinking and research that were involved in implementing an electronic reference service from the library's Web page and enhancing it with well-defined procedures and a plan for advertising the service. This article is a good resource for those contemplating adding an electronic reference to their library services.

PARTNERSHIPS

◀ Caspers, Jean S. **Outreach to Distance Learners: When the Distance Education Instructor Sends Students to the Library, Where Do They Go?** *Reference Librarian* 67/68 (1999): 299–311. Copublished simultaneously as *Library Outreach, Partnerships, and Distance Learning: Reference Librarians at the Gateway*, ed. Wendi Arant and Pixey Anne Mosely, 299–311. Binghamton, NY: Haworth Press, 2000.

Because outreach is crucial to providing successful distance education library services, librarians must play an active role in the distance education community. Caspers explores the ideas of librarians and outreach, as well as the processes of designing, marketing, and evaluating distance library services.

◀ Dugdale, Christine. **Academic/Librarianship Partnerships in the Electronic Library.** *Program* 33, no. 1 (1999): 15–28.

The many advantages of using electronic reserves are discussed and illustrated by the author's electronic reserves system of choice, ResIDE

Electronic Reserve. Dugdale also emphasizes the importance of the development of a partnership between academic and library staff. She believes that establishing closer working relations with the academic staff will result in the creation and exploitation of an electronic reserve, which will develop into a very important, effective, and flexible teaching/learning tool for students, academics, and librarians.

◀ Logue, Susan. **Instructive Support in the Changing Library Environment.** *Technical Services Quarterly* 17, no. 1 (1999): 13–22.

Librarians at Morris Library (Southern Illinois University, Carbondale) have met the challenge of changing to meet the needs of their users by increasing departmental partnerships and creating new resources and services through the use of new technology.

◀ Rader, Hannelore B. **A New Academic Library Model: Partnerships for Learning and Teaching.** *College and Research Libraries News* 62, no. 4 (2001): 393–96. Online. *WilsonSelectPlus_FT.* Article number BLIB01004561. (24 August 2001).

The librarians at the University of Louisville (UL) have entered into a variety of partnerships and have become more centered within the campus teaching and learning community. Rader describes these initiatives, which have enabled the libraries to become more visible both on campus and in the community and more involved in teaching, learning, and research. It is helpful and inspiring to see the positive outcomes from the partnerships UL has formed.

◀ Ury, Connie Jo, Joyce A. Meldrem, and Carolyn V. Johnson. **Academic Library Outreach Through Faculty Partnerships and Web-Based Research Aids.** *The Reference Librarian* 67/68 (1999): 243–56. Copublished simultaneously as *Library Outreach, Partnerships, and Distance Learning: Reference Librarians at the Gateway,* ed. Wendi Arant and Pixey Anne Mosely, 246–56. Binghamton, NY: Haworth Press, 2000.

The roles and workloads of academic librarians are shifting due to the continual evolution of electronic library services and online resources. The authors profile five trends that have affected the reference and instructional services offered by Owens Library at Northwest Missouri State University. Reallocation of staffing through a differentiated reference desk service model provides time to author curriculum-centered online research guides and tutorials, bibliographies, and Webliographies. It has also facilitated the development of a new and unique information service that partners information professionals with departmental faculty in a variety of subject areas. The authors report interesting solutions to a common problem.

NOTES

1.   Davis, Hazel M. Distance Learning Students and Library Services: Issues, Solutions, and the Rio Salado College Model. *Community and Junior College Libraries* 9, no. 2 (2000): 3–13.

2.   Kirk, Elizabeth E., and Andrea M Bartelstein. Libraries Close In on Distance Education. *Library Journal* 124, no. 6 (1999): 40–42. Online. Proquest. (14 March 2001).

3.   Dugdale, Christine. Academic/Librarianship Partnerships in the Electronic Library. *Program* 33, no. 1 (1999): 15–28.

4.   Caspers, Jean S. Outreach to Distance Learners: When the Distance Education Instructor Sends Students to the Library, Where Do They Go? *Reference Librarian* 67/68 (1999): 299–311. Copublished simultaneously as *Library Outreach, Partnerships, and Distance Learning: Reference Librarians at the Gateway,* ed. Wendi Arant and Pixey Anne Mosely, 299–311. Binghamton, NY: Haworth Press, 2000.

5.   Cutler, Kay A., Beth Blanton-Kent, and Judy Jordan. Going the Distance: Instructional and Reference Services in Distance Learning. *Virginia Libraries* 45, no. 1 (1999): 6–8.

Resources for Higher Education

ACCREDITATION

◄ **Handbook of Accreditation.** Chicago: NCA Commission on Institutions of Higher Education (CIHE), 1999. A publication from the NCA-CIHE to guide the accreditation process. Also available are the *2001 Addendum to the Handbook of Accreditation*[1] and *A Collection of Papers on Self-Study and Institutional Improvement, 2000*, 2000. http://www.ncahigherlearningcommission.org/resources/index.html (August 2001).

◄ **Manual for School Evaluation.** Bedford, MA: New England Association of Schools and Colleges (NEASC), 1999. An NEASC publication to guide self-study. Available in hard copy at http://www.neasc.org/cis /schl_eval.htm (August 2001).

◄ **1998 Criteria for Accreditation.** This is a document listing accreditation criteria (August 2001). Included are statements concerning distance learning. Available online through the Website of the Southern Association of Colleges and Schools. http://www.sacscoc.org /criteria.asp.

◄ **1999 Distance Education Handbook.** A publication of the Western Association of Schools and Colleges that includes accreditation concerns, distance learning through telecommunications, the *Principles of Good Practice for Electronically Delivered Academic Degree and Certificate Programs*, and guidelines for distance education accreditation standards. http://www.accjc.org/dislearn.htm (August 2001).

◄ **Policy Statement on the Review of Electronically Offered Degree Programs,** 2000. **Statement of the Regional Accrediting Commissions on the Evaluation of Electronically Offered Degree and Certificate Programs and Guidelines for the Evaluation of Electronically Offered Degree and Certificate Programs,** 2000. These documents are found at the Website of the Commission on Institutions of Higher Education. The policy statement on distance education and the interregional policy statement are guidelines for the evaluation of distance education. http://www.neasc.org/cihe/memo_evaluation_distance_education.htm (August 2001).

ASSOCIATIONS AND ORGANIZATIONS

A number of professional education and distance learning associations serve the higher education academic community in the United States. As more and more colleges and universities enter the distance education market, these associations have begun to provide information on distance education. This section includes a listing of the major organizations both in the United States and globally. This is not meant to be an inclusive listing. We include brief descriptions, important publications, and the URLs for those now on the Web. Many sites provide valuable links to distance learning research studies and resources.

American Association for Adult and Continuing Education (AAACE). AAACE is the nation's premier organization dedicated to enhancing the field of adult learning. Members are from secondary and postsecondary education, business and labor, military and government, and community-based organizations. The AAACE publishes *Adult Learning* and *Adult Education Quarterly.* http://www.aaace.org/.

American Association for Higher Education (AAHE). AAHE is an individual membership organization that promotes the changes higher education must make to ensure its effectiveness in a complex, interconnected world. Publications include the AAHE bulletin, *Powerful Partnerships: A Shared Responsibility for Learning*, which is a joint report from AAHE, the American College Personnel Association (ACPA), and the National Association of

Student Personnel Administrators (NASPA). The AAHE provides information on assessment, faculty roles and rewards, programs for the promotion of institutional change, quality initiatives, teaching initiatives, and the Teaching, Learning, and Technology (TLT) Group. AAHE also provides a discussion forum. http://www.aahe.org/.

American Council on Education (ACE). ACE is the nation's coordinating higher education association dedicated to the belief that equal educational opportunity and a strong higher education system are the cornerstones of a democratic society. More than 1,800 members include accredited, degree-granting colleges and universities from all sectors of higher education and other educational or education-related organizations. ACE provides the latest information on new legislation and policies affecting colleges and universities, ACE projects, and trends in higher education. http://www.acenet.edu/.

American Distance Education Consortium (ADEC). ADEC is an international consortium of state and land grant institutions providing economical distance education programs and services via the latest information technologies. The Website provides information on courseware tools, satellite resources, and Internet and electronic trends. http://www.adec.edu.

Asian Association of Open Universities. The goals of this association are to improve the cost-effectiveness of member institutions through the exchange of management information, teaching resources, and research; promote standards among distance educators; and facilitate cooperative efforts with regional and international bodies. http://www.ouhk.edu.hk/~AAOUNet/.

Association of Web-Based Learning (AWBL). AWBL provides a sample Web-based lesson and tools to facilitate the learning process. The sample lesson is meant to help users understand and experience the interactivity of a Web-based lesson and how it can be used. Lessons on topics such as phonics, study skills, business communication, *Huckleberry Finn*, algebra, U.S. history, and preparing for home ownership take about 20 minutes each. http://www.awbl.com/.

Consortium for Educational Technology for University Systems (CETUS). CETUS is a consortium of the State University of New York (SUNY), the California State University System, and the City University of New York (CUNY) that was formed to explore initiatives in technology-assisted teaching, learning, and research. http://www.calstatcla.edu/academic /infocomp/learning/teachcetus.htm.

Copyright Clearance Center (CCC). Established by authors, publishers, and users as the nonprofit Reproduction Rights Organization (RRO) for the United States, the CCC operates licensing systems that facilitate compliance with copyright laws and promotes the constitutional purposes of copyright, namely progress and creativity in the arts and sciences. Information can be found here on the electronic course content service, academic permission service, and other guidelines. http://www.copyright.com/.

Council for Higher Education Accreditation (CHEA). CHEA is the new voice of the nation's colleges and universities on all matters regarding accreditation. Established in 1996 as a nonprofit organization, CHEA also acts as the national policy center and clearinghouse on accreditation for the entire higher education community. This extensive community includes colleges and universities throughout the country, regional associations and higher education commissions that accredit schools and institutions across the country, national accrediting bodies for special-mission institutions, specialized groups that accredit specific disciplines and professions, and national higher education associations headquartered in Washington, D.C. http://www.chea.org/.

Distance Education Clearinghouse. The University of Wisconsin-Extension, its partners, and other UW institutions provide information and links to current articles, bibliographies and resources, certificate programs, networks, video, definitions, glossaries, instructional communications systems, and more. http://www.uwex.edu/disted/home.html/.

EDUCAUSE. CAUSE and Educom were consolidated to create EDUCAUSE (http://www.educause.edu/). This association provides an extensive collection of higher education information technology materials on the Web and is a primary research group providing statistics on distance learning and other distance learning documents or abstracts (http://www.educause .edu/page2/dist%5Flearning%5Fstats.html). EDUCAUSE links to information on topics such as awards and fellowships, collaborations, conferences and activities, current issues, information resources, job postings, and other publications—*CAUSE/EFFECT* and *Educom Review* at http://www.cause.org/. EDUCAUSE has its own discussion group. http://www.educause.edu/memdir /cg/cg.html/.

ERIC Clearinghouse on Higher Education. ERIC-HE is one of 16 clearinghouses funded by the Department of Education as a part of the Educational Resources Information Center (ERIC) system. The clearinghouse is also a sponsored research project for George Washington University. Their mission is "to improve American education by increasing and facilitating the use of education research and information on practice." ERIC-HE features the ASHE-ERIC report series, the Higher Education Library, online workshops, research initiatives and projects, and links to many resources. http://www .eriche.org/.

The Higher Learning Commission. The Higher Learning Commission of the North Central Association accredits colleges, universities, and other degree-granting institutions of higher education. http://www.ncahigherlearningcommission.org/index.html.

Institute for Information Literacy (IIL). The IIL, part of the Association for College and Research Libraries (ACRL), a division of the American Library Association, acts as a support mechanism for librarians, other educators, and administrators in developing and implementing information literacy programs. IIL developed the Information Literacy Competency Standards for Higher Education. Information literacy is common to all disciplines, learning environments, and levels of education and is relevant to lifelong learning. http://www.ala.org/acrl/nili/nilihp.html.

The International Association of Universities (IAU). IAU is a UNESCO-affiliated organization that was formally established in 1950 to encourage wide-reaching links among institutions of higher education. IAU is a worldwide organization with member institutions in approximately 150 countries that cooperate with a vast network of international, regional, and national bodies. This Website provides information on higher education worldwide and offers links to publications (e.g., *International Handbook of Universities*, World List of Universities and Other Institutions of Higher Education, *Higher Education Policy, Academic Quarterly Journal, Issues in Higher Education* [monograph series], and *IAU Newsletter)*, papers, reports, and resources. http://www.unesco.org/iau/.

The International Centre for Distance Learning (ICDL). ICDL is an international center for research, teaching, consultancy, information, and publishing activities affiliated with the Institute of Educational Technology. ICDL is an essential information resource covering more than 15 years of material in its distance education library and databases. The ICDL distance education databases contain information on more than 31,000 distance learning programs and courses from more than 1,000 institutions worldwide, mostly in the Commonwealth. More than 11,000 abstracts of books, journal articles, research reports, conference papers, dissertations, and other types of literature relating to all aspects of the theory and practice of distance education are available through ICDL. http://www-icdl.open.ac.uk/icdl/.

The International Council for Open and Distance Education (ICDE). The ICDE is a global membership organization of educational institutions from more than 130 countries, national and regional associations, corporations, educational authorities, and agencies in the fields of open learning, distance education, and flexible, lifelong learning. ICDE facilitates international cooperation in distance education and open learning throughout the world. http://www.icde.org.

International Literacy Institute (ILI). UNESCO and the University of Pennsylvania Graduate School of Education established ILI in 1994. ILI disseminates a newsletter and information on literacy innovations, research, development, training, and networking activities around the world. http://www.literacyonline.org/.

National University Continuing Education Association (NUCEA). NUCEA consists of more than 2,000 professional continuing educators at more than 410 accredited, degree-granting higher education institutions or nonprofit organizations. It is divided into seven geographic regions and promotes opportunities and high-quality continuing higher education. Each of the 20 NUCEA divisions and four caucuses focuses on a specific issue in continuing education, such as programs for older adults or administrative issues (e.g., marketing). NUCEA provides many publications for colleges, universities, and students including *The NUCEA News, The Electronic University, Lifelong Learning Trends, Peterson's Guide to 2001 Distance Learning Programs,* and *Peterson's Independent Study Catalog.* http://www.NUCEA.edu/.

Public Broadcasting Service (PBS). PBS is a private, nonprofit media enterprise owned and operated by the 348 public television stations in the United States. PBS uses the power of noncommercial television, the Internet, and other media to enrich the lives of Americans through quality programs and education services to nearly 100 million people each week. The PBS Adult Learning Service (ALS) (http://www.pbs.org/als/) is the nation's leading telecommunications-based service for higher education. ALS supports station-college partnerships providing formal and continuing education services, such as distance learning and for-credit college-level telecourses to more than 450,000 adult learners each year. In addition to college telecourses, the Adult Learning Satellite Service provides live, interactive videoconferences and resource programs ranging from literacy issues to professional development for faculty. http://www.pbs.org.

Software and Information Industry Association (SIIA). SIIA unites the software code and information content industries into a powerful global consortium. Its mission includes protecting the intellectual property of members, advocating a legal and regulatory environment for the entire industry, and serving as a resource. SIIA offers conferences, symposiums, and informal meetings on broad industry issues, views on software and information industry trends, and learning opportunities. http://www.siia.net/.

U.S. Department of Education. The department's mission is to ensure equal access to education and to promote educational excellence for all Americans as part of an effort to help the United States reach its national education goals. The following Website offers information about the department, including initiatives and priorities, grant opportunities, offices, publications, research, and statistics. http://www.ed.gov.

The United States Distance Learning Association (USDLA). The USDLA is a nonprofit association formed in 1987 to promote the development and application of distance learning for education and training. The association serves K–12 education, higher education, continuing education, corporate training, and military and government training in all 50 states. The USDLA developed and published a set of national policy recommendations that have been the basis of legislative and administrative proposals in education and telecommunications policy. http://www.usdla.org/.

WestEd Distance Learning Resource Network. WestEd is a nonprofit research, development, and service agency dedicated to improving education and other opportunities for children, youth, and adults. This organization addresses critical issues in education and related areas from early childhood intervention to school-to-work transition and from curriculum, instruction, and assessment to safe schools and communities. WestEd serves as the regional education laboratory for Arizona, California, Nevada, and Utah. Its headquarters are in San Francisco, with additional offices in Arizona, Massachusetts, Washington, D.C., and elsewhere in California. http://www.wested.org.

World Association for Online Education (WAOE). WAOE is an international professional organization concerned with online pedagogy. It offers membership services relevant to educators concerned with teaching online, public services for international society, and collaboration with other educational organizations functioning in cyberspace. http://waoe.org/.

LISTSERVS AND DISCUSSION GROUPS

A growing number of listservs and discussion groups serve the communication needs of the academic virtual learning environment. This list of selected groups is not inclusive and continues to grow each day. They are an excellent resource for keeping current with colleagues and other professionals on new developments and the issues concerning distance education and online learning.

Listservs

CETUS. http://www.cetus.org/fair8.html. A listserv for open discussion to help track developments and points of view regarding fair-use scenarios.

Distance Education Online Symposium (DEOS-L). An active listserv focusing on issues of distance learning with more than 2,000 participants from more than 50 countries. To join send an e-mail to listserv@psuvm.psu.edu with this message: subscribe DEOS-L Your Name.

Discussion Groups

This section provides brief descriptions of distance learning discussion groups. Groups both in the United States and other countries are identified here with their Web address and e-mail address. Although a few of the discussion groups are geared to educators K–12, the discussion of issues and resources is beneficial for future teachers and administrators also at the college level.

Am98 Online Course List. The Free Animation College's third online course for users of Hash, Inc.'s Animation: Master software. A syllabus can be found at http://www.geocities.com/SoHo/Atrium/4275. The eGroup address is: am98_class@eGroups.com.

College and University User Services Seminar List. A discussion list meant for educators and alumni dealing with computers and Internet resources. The eGroup address is: cuuss-l@listserv.acsu.buffalo.edu.

CSS Internet News Course Announcement. The CSS Internet News provides low-cost training by e-mail. The online learning series of courses is accessed through http://www.networx.on.ca/~jwalker/course.htm. To subscribe, send an empty message to on-line-learning-subscribe@makelit.com. The eGroup address is: on-line-learning@eGroups.com.

Distance Learning and Developing Countries. A discussion list for researchers, administrators, educators, and students interested in distance learning or distance education in developing countries. The e-Group address is: dldc@eGroups.com. Their Web address is http://www.egroups.com/group/dldc/fulinfo.html.

Distance Learning Interest Group. This group provides a forum for the discussion of the application of technologies to distance learning activities and the information environment. Members discuss the new roles of librarians serving distant users and distance learning activities at Southern Illinois University, Carbondale. To subscribe, send an empty message to: thunder.lib.siu.edu/lita/.

Education Resource List. This is a mailing list for education resources available on the Internet to Internet educators, teachers, and administrators. To subscribe, send an empty message to: edresource-subscribe@egroups.com.

EFI: Writing for Webheads. This is a discussion group for "Writing for Webheads," an English course. Students make Web pages and meet online occasionally. The eGroup address is: efiwebheads@eGroups.com.

European Association for Research on Learning and Instruction (EARLI). EARLI promotes the systematic exchange and discussion of ideas related to instructional and educational research, as well as research on industrial training. It serves more than 1,000 members in 40 countries. The e-Group address is: earli@hearn.nic.surfnet.nl.

GhaCLAD Education/Curriculum Development. The GhaCLAD Education and Curriculum Development Committee is a forum for discussion of local production of software and hardware; provision of technical services; promotion of wider public access; computer literacy and Internet training; adult literacy education; distance education at primary, secondary, and tertiary levels; local/indigenous knowledge building; the dissemination of information; and more. The eGroup address is: edu-curriculum@eGroups.com.

Ghana Computer Literacy and Distance Education (GhaCLAD) Discussion Forum. GhaCLAD is a not-for-profit corporation registered in Illinois. It was founded as an international, all-volunteer organization to ensure that countries throughout Africa, particularly Ghana, are able to take their place in the information and communication age. The eGroup address is: ghaclad-discussion @eGroups.com.

Ghana WorLD Project. This group is involved in collaborative projects (e.g., the World Bank World Links for Development Project) linking secondary schools in Ghana to other schools worldwide. For more information go to http://www.world-links.org/ghana/ or http://www.worldbank.org/html/schools /wlinks.htm. The eGroup address is: ghanaschools@eGroups.com.

Information Technology Teaching. IT Teaching Today is an information group in the United Kingdom for those who teach educators and administrators about information technology. The eGroup address is: it_teaching@eGroups .com. To subscribe, send an empty message to: it_teaching-subscribe@egroups .com.

Innovative Teaching at the Surfaquarium. This newsletter is designed for teachers to keep them up to date with Internet resources on a weekly topic. The eGroup address is: innovative-teaching@eGroups.com.

Intellectual Property Group (IPG) Discussion List. The IPG is a student organization at Boston College Law School. Its purpose is to promote discussion on IPG activities, events, and intellectual property-related legal issues (e.g., trademark, patent, copyright, trade secrets, computer law, and entertainment law). The eGroup address is: ipg@admin1.bc.edu.

Legal and Ethical Internet Issues. This is a discussion list for teachers interested in the legal and ethical issues surrounding teaching with the Internet. The eGroup address is: legaleth@eGroups.com. To subscribe, send an empty message to: legaleth-subscribe@egroups.com.

Libraries and Distance Learning. This discussion group comes out of the Chancellor's Office Plan for Equity of Student and Faculty Access to Quality Library and Learning Resources Programs in the California Community Colleges. The focus is on the role of the library in supporting distance learning. The eGroup address is: http://groups.yahoo.com/group/librariesanddistancelearning.

Outstudents. This is a mailing list for Open University students. The eGroup address is: outstudents@eGroups.com.

Palmer Library School Summer 1998 Class. This discussion group promotes communication between class members and Professor Terry Ballard for the course "Access and Management of Web Resources." To subscribe, send an empty message to: lis901-subscribe@makelist.com. The eGroup address is: lis901@eGroups.com.

Pelican 1B Course Information. Pelican_1B is a specific class informational e-mail list supporting English 1B, "Writing About the Environment." The eGroup address is: pelican_1b@eGroups.com.

Privacy in Cyberspace Section 1. This is an e-mail group list for Section 1 of Privacy in Cyberspace and the online lecture and discussion series sponsored by Harvard Law School. The eGroup address is: privacyolad-sec1@eGroups.com.

Simcoe Cyber Selections. These selections are an interactive sourcing of URLs for use in classrooms, sharing of units and classroom ideas, and professional development announcements for teachers and teacher librarians in Simcoe County and beyond. The eGroup address is: Simcoe_selections@eGroups.com.

Smart Schools Initiative. The Smart School Initiative is a project launched by Smart Valley, Inc., to bring the Internet and information technology into K–12 schools through a partnership with the San Jose Education Network. The eGroup address is: smartschools@svi.org.

SUNY Faculty Access to Computing Technology Discussion List. The eGroup address for this discussion list is: fact-l@listserv.acsu.buffalo.edu.

Technology Educators. This is a private listserv for technology educators and coordinators in the Arkansas-Louisiana-Mississippi area. It provides lesson plan ideas and resources. To subscribe, send an empty message to: areatech_net-subscribe@egroups.com or go to the e-group's home page at http://www.egroups.com/list/areatech_net.

UtahLINK. The UtahLINK World Wide Web listserv connects Utah educators and administrators who use the Web for teaching, creating WWW pages, communication, and solving problems involving educational issues. The eGroup address is: utlink-www@uen.org.

Virtual District. This is a discussion group for professional educators involved in a distance learning project involving five Texas school districts using Web-facilitated learning and two-way interactive videoconferencing through ISDN lines. To subscribe, send a message to: virtual-district-subscribe @egroups.com or go to the group's home page at http://www.egroups.com /list/virtual-district. The eGroup address is: virtual-district@eGroups.com.

The World Association for Online Education (WAOE). WAOE is an association that looks at the challenges of online organization and collaboration in the development of global, online learning. It is a virtual association of professionally based members who might never meet face to face. Decisions and meeting participation are carried out online. The e-Group address is waoe-views@waoe.org. WAOE's Web address is http://www.egroups.com /group/waoe-views/info.html.

JOURNALS AND NEWSLETTERS

This section identifies selected journals and newsletters relating to distance learning or distance education found in the traditional format and online. URLs are included for online journals. The titles we include cover publications both in the United States and around the world.

The American Journal of Distance Education (AJDE). Contains articles, interviews, and reviews on current information related to various aspects of distance education. The *AJDE* contents, author guidelines, and more, as well as other distance education publications are listed on the Website. Published by the American Center for the Study of Distant Education, University Park, PA. ISSN 0892-3647. http://www.ed.psu.edu/ACSDE/.

COMLEARN. A publication of the Commonwealth of Learning in Canada.

Communiqué. Published six times a year by the Canadian Association for Distance Education. ISSN 0884-3643.

Consortium International Francophone de Formation à Distance (CIFFAD). Published in France. ISSN 0164-534X. This French speaking institute provides information on the formation of new information technologies. The text appears in French. However, the text can be translated into English by searching "Consortium International Franciphone de Formation a Distance" through the http://www.google.com search engine.

DEANZ Bulletin. A publication of the Distance Education Association of New Zealand.

DEOSNEWS. An online journal published by the Distance Education Online Symposium at Pennsylvania State University. Publishes articles on distance education topics worldwide. ISSN 1062-9416.

Distance Education and Technology Newsletter. Publishes articles on distance education and educational technology in the United States and worldwide. ISSN 1064-2439.

Distance Education and Training Network Newsletter. Published quarterly by the Distance Education and Training Network of the National Society for Performance and Instruction (NSPI), Canada.

Distance Education Research Update Newsletter (DERUN). Published twice a year by the Division for Distance and Continuing Education (DDCE) at Central Queensland University in Australia. Also available online at http://www.online.ddce.cqu.edu.au/derun/start.html.

The Distance Educator. A quarterly newsletter reporting on distance learning. ISSN 1084-6972. http://www.distance-educator.com/.

Distant Education. A peer-reviewed journal published twice a year by the Open and Distance Learning Association of Australia. ISSN 0158-7979.

Distant Education Report. A quarterly publication covering distance learning topics. ISSN 1094-320X.

DLA Newsletter. Published by the Distance Learning Association (DLA) of Southern Africa.

EADTU. A newsletter published by the European Association of Distance Teaching Universities in the Netherlands.

ED: The Official Publication of the United States Distance Learning Association (USDLA). OCLC 19231745. See also, *Education at a Distance: ED.*

EDEN Newsletter. Published by the European Distance Education Network in the United Kingdom.

Education at a Distance: ED. Published by the USDLA. Provides articles on distance education and telecommunications in the United States. OCLC 41306226.

EDUCAUSE Quarterly. Formerly *CAUSE/EFFECT.* A practitioner's journal covering topics related to managing and using information resources on college and university campuses. ISSN 1528-5324. http://www.educause.edu /pub/eq/eq.html.

First Monday. Publishes articles about the Internet and the global information infrastructure. Articles review standards, Internet content, use, and regulatory and political issues and reviews research on the development of software and hardware for the Internet. ISSN 1396-0466. http://firstmonday .org.

Global E-Learning News (GEN). A monthly newsletter covering the emerging global markets for North American marketed postsecondary education. It provides information on how to enter and excel in the global Internet-enabled adult education market. http://www.geteducated.com/gen/gen.htm. E-mail: gen@geteducated.com.

INFocus. A newsletter reporting on innovative continuing education programs in U.S. higher education institutions and related topics for professionals.

Interactive Multimedia Electronic Journal of Computer-Enhanced Learning (IMEJ of CEL). *IMEJ* is a peer-reviewed interactive multimedia electronic journal edited and produced by Wake Forest University. It acts as a forum for innovations in computer-enhanced learning. Articles cover topics ranging from designing a course for media delivery and studying the effects of learning styles in a multimedia environment to using interactive Web tools in teaching. http://imej.wfu.edu/.

Issues in Science and Technology Librarianship. A quarterly published by the Association of College and Research Library (ACRL) Science and Technology Section. It serves as a vehicle for sci-tech librarians to share details of successful programs, materials for the delivery of information services, background information, opinions on topics of current interest, research and bibliographies. ISSN 1092-1206. http://www.library.ucsb.edu/istl/.

Istruzione a Distanza (IAD). Published quarterly in Italy. It is published in Italian, but the scope is international.

Journal for Interactive Media in Education (JIME). A peer-reviewed on-line journal (e-journal) meant for practitioners, system designers, policy makers, and researchers involved in educational technology. This unique journal provides a document interface that allows readers to access secondary resources, interactive demonstrations, video and audio clips, instruments for evaluation, and discussion groups. An excellent article appearing in *First Monday* describes this publication and provides illustrations demonstrating its interactivity.[2]

The Journal of Asynchronous Learning Networks (JALN). JALN is published online by Vanderbilt University for the ALN Web. It provides scholarly research for practitioners in the field of asynchronous learning networks. The ALN Web also contains *ALN Magazine* (similar articles with links to other sites, materials, columns, news, and workshops). The *JALN* provides viewable and downloadable journal articles in the format of a traditional journal. ISSN 1092-8235. http://www.aln.org/alnweb/journal/jaln.htm or http://www.aln .org/alnweb/magazine/maga_v3_i2.htm.

Journal of Distance Education. Published twice a year by the Canadian Association for Distance Education (CADE). Promotes scholarly and empirical information relating to distance education in Canada. ISSN 0839-0445.

The Journal of Distance Learning. A peer-reviewed journal published by the Distance Education Association of New Zealand.

Journal of Library Services for Distance Education (JLSDE). JLSDE is a peer-reviewed online journal serving the needs of distance education students and faculty, who are looking for library support. ISSN 1096-2123. http://www .westga.edu/~library/jlsde/.

Kakatiya Journal of Distance Education. Published twice a year by the School of Distance Learning and Continuing Education at Kakatiya University, Warangal, India.

ODLAA Times. Published by the Open and Distance Learning Association of Australia. ISSN 1320-7954.

Online Chronicle of Distance Education and Communication. Published twice a year by Nova Southeastern University in Florida to create a network of distance education practitioners. Subscribe via e-mail to LISTPROC@PULSAR .ACAST.NOVA.EDU. In the subject type DISTED and your name within the body of message.

Online Journal of Distance Learning Administration. Quarterly publication of the original work of practitioners and researchers with specific focus on or implications for the management of distance education programs. Articles cover topics of interest to administration (e.g., distance program planning and implementation, online delivery applications, distance instructor training and support, technology, IT leadership, Web-based course models, copyright law, and expectations for the future of distance learning). OCLC 39254. http://www.westga.edu/~distance/jmain11.html.

Open Forum: Distance Education and Open Learning. Articles reflect current theory, practice, and research related to distance education and open learning systems. Published in Australia.

Open Learning. Publishes book reviews and peer-reviewed theoretical and practice-based articles reflecting global developments in distance, flexible, and open education and training. Published three times a year in the United Kingdom. The primary audience is those involved in postsecondary education. ISSN 0268-0513. http://www.tandf.co.uk/journals/carfax/02680513.html.

The Quarterly Review of Distance Education. Published by Nova Southwestern University in Florida. ISSN 1528-3518.

Research in Distance Education Quarterly. Published by the Center for Distance Education at Athabasca University. ISSN 0843-8854.

Revista de Educación a Distancia. A Spanish publication that includes articles from around the world. Published three times a year in Spain.

Revista Iberoamericana de Educación Superior a Distancia. Published three times a year. Articles cover information and reviews from member institutions. ISSN 0214-3992.

Using Telematics in Education and Training. Published ten times a year in the United Kingdom. Provides current information on technology-based education.

Virtual University Business Digest (VUBD). A monthly news digest published for entrepreneurs, deans, and executives who are building Internet-enabled, for-profit, e-education enterprises for the adult market. Covers topics such as new partnerships, alliances, and acquisitions, as well as trends in marketing, product development, and delivery. http://www.geteducated.com /vubd/vubd.htm. E-mail: vubd@geteducated.com.

The Virtual University Gazette. A monthly e-mail newsletter published for those involved in developing, administering, or delivering online or computer-mediated distance education for the adult education and training markets. *The Virtual University Gazette* is published by geteducated.com, a distance education consulting, research, and industry watch firm working with colleges and corporations. *The Virtual University Business Digest* and *Global E-Learning News* are also published online at http://www.geteducated.com. and http://www.yarranet.net.au/aceweb/mailarch/00000107.htm.

Virtual University Journal. A quarterly journal from England. ISSN 1460-7441.

MEDIA

The following section provides a selective list of media that cover various aspects of distance learning. These include videocassettes, sound recordings, and machine-readable data.

◀ Altes, Jand, Leah Fleming, Kim Caitlyn, et al. **Work in Your Life; Returning Women in College; Distance Learning; Efficient Sex? Suffragettes.** 25 minutes. Troy, NY: Sage College, Albany. WAMC Public Radio, 1999. OCLC 42255779. Audiocassette.

This radio program reviews studies of women returning to college and their experiences with lack of time and self-confidence. This first part of a series of broadcasts looks at how higher education can address their needs through distance learning.

◀ **Building a Presence on the Web.** RMI Media Productions. Videocassette.

◀ **CU-SeeMe Pro.** Nashua, NH: White Pine Software, 1999. Machine-readable data.

This videoconferencing software program for the desktop computer features color video, audio, chat, and data sharing. It can be used with the Internet or any TCP/IP network for real-time, person-to-person or group conferencing, broadcasts, and chats. System requirements include an Internet connection with an IP address; 10MB hard disk space; modem speed of 33.6bps or faster for dial-up connections; Pentium processor, 133MHz; 32MB RAM: Microsoft Windows 95, 98, or Windows NT 4.0. For H.232 collaboration, Pentium 166MHz, 64MB RAM, and 56Lbps modem speed are recommended.

◀ **Distance Learning: The Next Century.** Federal Emergency Management Agency Teleconference (29 January 1992), Emmitsburg, MD. 144 minutes. Capitol Heights, MD: National Audiovisual Center, 1992. OCLC 26978217. Videocassette.

This video discusses distance learning technologies, learning networks, innovative low-cost teaching experiments, and successful learning projects.

◀ **Distance Learning Today.** 30 minutes. St. Paul: MnSAT and St. Paul Technical College, 1996. Videocassette.

A broadcast on 7 March 1996. Defines distance learning and explains the need to expand it.

◀ **Distance Learning Today: Legal Issues.** 120 minutes. St. Paul: MnSAT, 1998. OCLC 39390605. Videocassette.

This video was broadcast in March 1997 and taped from a satellite transmission on 11 May 1998. It covers licensing rights through the PBS Adult Learning Satellite Service. It discusses legal issues involving the use of copyrighted works for distance education, the protection of the rights of intellectual property owners, fair use and its application, and future trends that will affect distance learning.

◀ **Distance Learning Today Series: An Introduction.** RMI Media Productions. Videocassette.

◀ Huband, Frank. **The Virtual University: Alternatives to Traditional Structures.** 90 minutes. Scientia Colloquium Series, 2000. OCLC 44003125. Videocassette.

This lecture, sponsored by Scientia, was held at Rice University, 18 January 2000. The discussion centers on the future of distance learning in higher education and ways in which technology will transform teaching and learning.

◀ **Interactive Learning Environments.** RMI Media Productions. Videocassette.

◄ **Introduction to Legal Issues.** C. J. Braaten, 26 minutes. St. Paul: Minnesota Satellite and Technology, 1997. OCLC 40096008. Videocassette.

Provides an overview of issues and questions from educators about copyright and distance learning.

◄ **Methods and Mediums.** RMI Media Productions. Videocassette.

◄ **The 1998 TLA Annual Conference.** Texas Library Association Conference, San Antonio 1998. San Diego: The Sound of Knowledge, 1998. OCLC 40349992. Eight audiocassettes.

Discusses distance learning and information services and outsourcing services for the library.

◄ **On-Line Course Delivery.** RMI Media Productions. Videocassette.

◄ **The Power of Distance Learning.** 11 minutes. New York: NYTel Corporate Television, 1994. OCLC 35092807. Videocassette.

Educational administrators address the issue of distance learning in the diverse parts of New York state.

◄ **Protecting Intellectual Property.** C. J. Braaten. 28 minutes. St. Paul: Minnesota Satellite and Technology, 1997. OCLC 40095902. Videocassette.

This video points out the differences between copyrights, trademarks, and patents. It reviews the protection of intellectual property and discusses the issue of transferring information across international borders via the Internet.

◄ **Real Time Communications via the Internet.** Richard Wiggins. 54 minutes. East Lansing: Michigan State University (MSU), 1996. OCLC 41485786. Videocassette.

Broadcast on 4 December 1996 on ITV Cable, this video addresses the possibilities for and limitations of various Internet-based real-time communications schemes now in use at MSU and globally. It reviews text-based conferencing tools such as Internet Relay Chat and Netscape Chat; Internet telephone applications such as Netscape and Cooltalk; Internet videophone applications such as CU-SeeMe; and share whiteboard applications and streaming audiovisual applications such as Xing and RealAudio.

◀ **Technology and How It Affects Intellectual Property.** Joan Steffend. 29 minutes. St. Paul: Minnesota Satellite and Technology, 1997. OCLC 36870308. Videocassette.

Discusses distance learning technology issues such as copyrighted works for distance education, protecting the rights of intellectual property owners, fair use and its application to distance learning, and future trends.

◀ Thomas, Lorna, Michelle Halsell, and Regina Taylor. **Virtual Equality: The Information Revolution and the Inner City.** Produced and directed by Lorna Thomas. 58 minutes. Princeton: Films for the Humanities and Sciences, 2000. OCLC 44846442. Videocassette.

This video is one of four in a series presented as a segment in the PBS television series, the *Digital Divide*. This segment examines the various issues raised by new technologies and the Internet, such as the effect of the technologies on classroom learning, as well who has access to the technology. The video focuses on the need for technology-centered education in higher education and community technology centers. The viewpoints of teachers, government, and students are expressed.

◀ **The Third Annual Distance Learning Conference.** Pomona: Distance Learning Conference at California State Polytechnic University, 1996. Videocassette.

◀ **The Tidal Wave Is Coming: Virtual Universities; Screenagers; College Survival in the Technology Era.** Doreen Dailey. Santa Clarita, CA: Professional Programs, 1995. OCLC 40189903. Audiocassette.

This video presents the effect of technological innovations (e.g., the information superhighway and Internet) and telecommunications on higher education.

◀ **Video Conferencing Classroom.** 98 minutes. Lock Haven, PA: Center for Distance Education, Pennsylvania State System of Higher Education, 1999. OCLC 41643875. Videocassette.

Describes classroom arrangements, equipment, and instructional strategies that work well in a videoconferencing environment.

◀ **Videoconferencing Terms.** Toby Trowt-Bayard. Corona Del Mar, CA: Videoconference.com, 1997. Machine-readable data.

A glossary of videoconferencing terms that can be accessed through the Internet. http://www.videoconference.com/glossary.htm.

◀ **Virtual Universities California Style**. Robert Threlkeld and John Reynolds. 88 minutes. Ferns: California State University, Fresno, 1997. OCLC 36947297. Videocassette.

A teleconference originating on 15 May 1997. This panel discussion presents an overview of the plans and scope of the California Virtual University.

◀ **Virtual Universities Online and On-Target?** Produced by Dallas TeleLearning, Dallas Teleconferences. 90 minutes. LeCroy Center for Educational Telecommunications, Dallas County Community College District, 2000. OCLC 43420805. Videocassette.

This video features a teleconference that was made up of a moderator and panelists from virtual universities discussing their own initiatives in distance education. Panel members discuss the following questions: What is the effect of distance education from virtual universities on traditional colleges and universities? How successful are their efforts and mission? Are virtual universities changing the face of higher education, or are they distorting it?

◀ **VTEL**. 11 minutes, 50 seconds. Austin: VTEL, 1996. OCLC 43271926. Videocassette.

Reviews interactive learning through videoconferencing.

WEBSITES

The following section selectively lists Websites that provide information and resources on distance learning, distance learning degree programs, and additional distance learning links.

AcademicNet
http://www.academic.com/

This site is Web-based content, tools, and services created by Academic Systems. It provides information resources for educators interested in technology-mediated instruction and roundtables—online discussion groups for faculty. It also provides a selection of online resources for higher education that includes an electronic library of articles, papers, and speeches about technology-mediated instruction and learning, plus links to other online resources useful to those interested in technology and instruction, as well as links for higher education and instructional technology resources.

Accredited Distance Learning Degrees
http://www.accrediteddldegrees.com

This Website offers fully accredited degrees. Visitors can choose from more than 500 U.S. colleges and universities offering more than 900 degree fields. Distance education degrees include Bachelor's, Master's, doctoral, law, and MBA.

Distance Education Research
http://www.distancelearn.about.com/education/distancelearn
/library/weekly/aa021400a.htm

This Website provides links to sites on a variety of distance education research topics and resources including: "No Significant Difference" (effectiveness of distance instruction vs. classroom instruction); "Distance Education and the Digital Divide" (issues of information technology access); "Distance Learning Money Issues"; statistics; and recent calls for papers and conference presentations.

Distance Education Website
http://www.hofstra.edu/Libraries/Axinn/axinn_elresorc_disted.cfm

Provides connections to distance education resources under the following categories: general information, instruction, libraries and distance education, directories, organizations, higher education, publications technology, policy/planning/assessment, diploma "mills," and conferences. All site listings are annotated.

Eduspear
http://eduspear.com/

This site is a source of distance education news and resources. It includes a custom keyword searchable directory and topics such as the most popular distance sites, new distance learning sites, colleges, commercial programs, books, educators, free training, and miscellaneous resources.

Globewide Network Academy
http://www.gnacademy.org/

An educational nonprofit organization with a course and program catalog that is a comprehensive directory of distance learning opportunities throughout the world. The student channel contains links to resources of interest to distance learning students, and the teacher channel contains links to resources of interest to distance learning teachers.

Issues in Distance Education Websites—Rebecca Bock
http://www2.msstate.edu/~bock/websiteside.html

Links to information about adult learners, assessment, instructor-led courseware, certification training, and multimedia.

Library Support for Distance Learning—Bernie Sloan
http://alexia.lis.uiuc.edu/~b-sloan/libdist.htm

This site is primarily aimed at librarians interested in issues of library support for distance learners. It provides links to learning, regional initiatives, and planning/policy documents. It also provides selected papers on general issues in distance learning, library-specific meta-information on distance learning, selected papers and reports on library support for distance learning, state and regional Websites for library support for distance learning, individual library Websites for distance learning support, and selected papers on electronic reference services and evaluating Web resources.

Link-Systems International, Inc.
www.link-systems.com/

Link-Systems International provides integrated distance learning, Web publishing, and data conversion solutions to organizations worldwide. They specialize in the communication of mathematical, scientific, technical, and medical material. Their primary focus is on the development and licensing of tools that expedite the delivery of educational and training content over the Internet, both synchronously and asynchronously. Educational services include custom programming, textbook Websites, content development, and online tutoring.

Media Cottage
http://www.mediacottage.com/

Media Cottage is a multidisciplinary educational communication firm that specializes in presentation facility design, video and multimedia production, and telecommunication systems installation. This Website provides links to distance learning sites and the sites of professional organizations in communications, education resources, and online publications.

New Horizons for Learning
http://www.newhorizons.org/

New Horizons is an international, nonprofit educational network. Its functions include conferences, seminars, publications, an online journal, online classes, e-mail, listservs, discussion groups, links, and networking and referrals.

Online Teaching and Distance Learning
http://www.page-designs.com/office/teaching.html

Various links to distance education degree programs and courses worldwide, as well as distance education resources.

PBS—Distance Learning Week
http://www.pbs.org/als/dlweek/index.html

Provides a variety of distance learning information. Visitors can read about the history of distance learning from the 1800s to the present, peruse a glossary of distance learning terms, assess whether or not distance learning can fit their circumstances and lifestyles, discover innovative distance learning opportunities that are available in their communities, take a quiz testing their distance learning knowledge, and take a look at a plethora of resources on issues in distance learning.

Peterson's Distance Learning
http://iiswinprd03.petersons.com/distancelearning/default.asp

Visitors to this Website can search for distance learning programs (more than 3,600) by name, keyword, or degree or for more than 16,000 courses. In addition, visitors can discover if distance learning is right for you, learn about education financing options, and read distance education news and feature articles.

University Links: Distance Learning
http://www-net.com/univ/list/distance.html

This site provides a short list of U.S. colleges and universities that offer distance education courses. A search engine is also available.

Websites: Distance Education
www.studentaffairs.com/web/distan.html

This site provides a short list of distance education links. Each listing contains a separate review that has a direct link to the aforementioned site.

World Wide Web Virtual Library: Distance Education
http://www.cisnet.com/~cattales/Deducation.html

This site provides links to schools, distance learning organizations, distance learning resources, journals, articles, newsletters, and newsgroups.

Yahoo Distance Education Page
http://www.yahoo.com/Education/Distance_Learning/

This site provides an annotated list of links covering a variety of distance education topics.

NOTES

1. *Addendum to the Handbook of Accreditation,* 2d ed., 2001. Available from the Web in PDF format at http://www.ncahigherlearningcommission .org/resources/HandAddend.pdf (7 August 2001).

2. Shum, Buckingham, and Dimon and Tamara Sumner. JIME: An Interactive Journal for Interactive Media. *First Monday* 6, no. 2 (February 2001). http.//firstmonday.org/issue6_2/buckingham_shum/index.html.

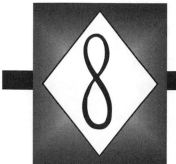

Additional Resources for Higher Education

The following list of additional resources is for planners, administrators, educators, instructors, and students and includes handbooks, guides, and directories of distance learning programs, yearbooks, and other resources. Abstracts are provided when the sources were available. Many of the citations in this section address one or more of the topics found elsewhere in this book. They provide good overviews of distance learning and related issues.

RESOURCES

◀ Armstrong, Myrna L. **Telecommunications for Health Professionals: Providing Successful Distance Education and Telehealth.** New York: Springer, 1998. ISBN 0826198406.

This handbook is for heath care professionals who need to create or manage programs in distance learning and patient care. Part I of the book examines distance education for continuing and academic programs. The chapters address issues such as undergraduate, graduate, and doctoral education; faculty and student issues; and library and communication support services. Part II presents the use of telecommunications for consolidating direct client health care services by means of a TeleHealth system. Part III discusses ethical, legal, and legislative concerns.

◀ Bear, John, and Mariah Bear. **Bears' Guide to Earning Degrees Nontraditionally**, 14th ed. Berkeley: Ten Speed Press, 2000. ISBN 1580082025.

This guide provides information on night and weekend colleges, foreign medical schools, Internet degrees, and other means to degrees by nontraditional methods. The Bears' Website is http://www.degree.net.

◀ Bear, John, and Mariah Bear. **Bears' Guide to the Best Education Degrees by Distance Learning**. Berkeley: Ten Speed Press, 2001. ISBN 1580083331.

This is a guide to distance learning degrees. It profiles colleges and universities and provides pertinent information.

◀ Bear, John, and Mariah Bear. **Bears' Guide to the Best MBAs by Distance Learning**. Berkeley: Ten Speed Press, 2000. ISBN 1580082203.

The Bears' book describes distance learning as an alternative way to earn an MBA. The authors cover topics such as financing, scholarships, degree mills, licensing laws, accredited or nonaccredited schools, and other important information on courses or programs. The Bears' Website is http://www.degree.net.

◀ Bear, John, and Mariah Bear. **College Degrees by Mail and Internet: 100 Accredited Schools That Offer Bachelor's, Master's, Doctorates, and Law Degrees by Distance Learning**. Berkeley: Ten Speed Press, 2001. ISBN 1580082173.

Updated each year, this book provides information on the latest trends in distance learning and lists the best schools, their profiles, and additional information (e.g., their Websites and e-mail addresses).

◀ Bear, John, Mariah Bear, and Tom C. Head. **Bears' Guide to Earning Degrees by Distance Learning**, 14th ed. Berkeley: Ten Speed Press, 2001. ISBN 1580082025.

Profiles regionally accredited schools, evening and weekend colleges, and foreign medical schools that offer Bachelor's, Master's, doctoral, and law degrees. It includes information on diploma mills and other schools to avoid.

◀ Boaz, Mary. **Teaching at a Distance: A Handbook for Instructors**. Mission Viejo, CA: League for Innovation in the Community College, Archipelago Productions, 1999. OCLC 42190355.

This handbook serves as a reference tool and a resource guide for distance education instructors. It presents fundamental ideas for designing, implementing, and facilitating courses for distance learning and examines topics that range from delivery technologies and collaboration to testing and evaluation methodologies. A section on "lessons learned" provides insight and wisdom for others by listing things that have succeeded or failed. A list of Web resources and a glossary are included in this valuable resource for faculty.

◀ Burgess, W. E. **The Oryx Guide to Distance Learning: A Comprehensive Listing of Correspondence, Electronic, and Media-Assisted Courses**, 3d ed. Phoenix: Oryx Press, 2000. OCLC 31622120.

Information about more than 700 institutions that provide 6,000 distance learning and correspondence courses.

◀ Clark, Tom, and David Else. **Distance Education, Electronic Networking, and School Policy.** Bloomington, IN: Phi Delta Kappa Education Foundation, 1998. ISBN 0873676416.

Though intended as a brief resource guide for K–12 school administrators, teachers, and policy makers, this book will be a good beginning resource for those in higher education who are dealing with distance learning and electronic networking policy issues. This book examines the roles of the federal, state, and local governments; planning and policy making; working with vendors, contractors and consultants; and emerging issues such as distributed learning, learning communities, and virtual schools and their influence on future policy issues.

◀ Cole, Robert A. **Issues in Web-Based Pedagogy: A Critical Primer.** Westport, CT: Greenwood Press, 2000. ISBN 0313312265.

As the title states, this book takes a critical look at Web-based pedagogy. Divided into two parts, the book presents essays that assess the form and content of Web-based instruction, both quantitatively and qualitatively. Part I focuses on the philosophical and theoretical considerations of Web-based pedagogy. The focal point of Part II is empirical and practical considerations. This work should be on everyone's beginning reading list about this subject.

◀ **Complete Book of Distance Learning Schools.** New York: Princeton Review Publishing Corporation, 2000. ISBN 0375762043.

Provides pertinent information on a number of schools that offer distance learning.

◀ Criscito, Pat. **Barron's Guide to Distance Learning Degrees, Certificates, Courses**. Hauppauge, NY: Barron's Educational Series, 2002. ISBN 0764117912.

This resource lists various types of distance learning programs and profiles accredited colleges and universities throughout the United States and Canada. The book lists degrees, certificates, and courses for undergraduate, graduate, and doctoral programs. The author provides the reader with background knowledge on distance learning, its history, methods (e.g., virtual classrooms and video and audio conferences), and interactive television. Important topics for potential students and educators are covered as well, such as accreditation, assessment, examinations, learning contracts, transcripts and grades, course materials, financing the cost with federal grants and scholarships, and financial resources on the Internet.

◀ **DegreeSearch, Training/Degree Programs, Over 8,000 Colleges.** Denver: ArchiveSolutions, 2000. http://www.degreesearch.com.

This is an online college directory search engine for students and administrators. It allows searching by state, program type (e.g., certificate, associate, bachelors, graduate, combined, distance), and institute type (e.g., public or private).

◀ Feyten, Carine M., and Joyce W. Nutta. **Virtual Instruction: Issues and Insights from an International Perspective**. Englewood, CO: Libraries Unlimited, 1999. ISBN 1563087146.

This resource reviews virtual instruction from a global perspective. The authors cover topics such as assessing cost-effectiveness; educational vision, theory, and technology for virtual learning; videoconferencing in education and training; examples from Asia and Japan; and cultural and linguistic diversity.

◀ Freeman, Howard, Bernard Scott, Daxa Patel, and Steve Ryan. **The Virtual University: The Internet and Resource-Based Learning**. Sterling, VA: Stylus, 2000. ISBN 0749425083.

The authors provide practical information for online instructors on resource-based learning, the role of technology, computer-generated learning, and communication on the Internet.

◀ Gibson, Chere Campbell. **Distance Learners in Higher Education: Institutional Responses for Quality Outcomes**. Madison, WI: Atwood, 1998. ISBN 1891859234.

A thorough introduction to distance education research, pertinent journals, and important issues for administrators, faculty, and students.

◀ Gilbert, Sarah Dulaney. **How to Be a Successful Online Student.** New York: McGraw-Hill, 2000. ISBN 0071365125.

A guide for students who would like to participate in distance learning. It reviews the technology and computer skills needed for using distance learning and the Internet.

◀ **Guide to Distance Learning Programs in the USA, 2001 Edition.** New Providence, NJ: R. R. Bowker, Reed Elsevier, 2001. ISBN 1894122941.

This resource highlights a variety of distance learning opportunities available in the United States—from undergraduate programs to certificate and short courses.

◀ Keith, Harry. **Higher Education Through Open and Distance Learning.** New York: Routledge, 1999. ISBN 0415197910.

Keith provides a world review of distance and open learning in higher education. This book brings together global distance learning experiences for community developers, politicians, policy makers, international development agencies, and others in the field. Some of the book's themes deal with costs, the internationalization of higher education, and the impact of technology. Africa, America, Asia, Europe, and Oceania are represented in the research.

◀ Krebs, Arlene. **The Distance Learning Funding Sourcebook: A Guide to Foundation, Corporate and Government Support for Telecommunications and the New Media.** Dubuque, IA: Kendall-Hunt, 1999. ISBN 0787249807.

This directory is designed for educators to identify key funding programs and grant-making agencies for financing online education projects such as Website construction, two-way videoconferencing, satellite broadcasts, and courseware creation. The directory provides descriptions of these programs; their priorities; grants they have awarded; and names, phone numbers, and e-mail addresses of contact people. It also includes helpful budget worksheets, sample request letters, and grant application forms.

◀ Lau, Sau, Raymond Boggs, and Jack Rochester. **Online Distance Learning in Higher Education, 1998–2002.** Framingham, MA: International Data.OCLC 43608069.

Reviews the use of computer-assisted instruction and the Internet in distance education in the United States.

◀ Lee, William, and Diana Owens. **Multimedia-Based Instructional Design, Computer-Based Training, Web-Based Training, and**

Distance Learning. San Francisco: Jossey-Bass, 2000. ISBN 0787951595.

Describes the use of multimedia in distance education through the Internet along with computer-assisted instruction.

◀ Mantyla, Karen. **Interactive Distance Learning Exercises That Really Work**. Alexandria, VA: American Society for Training and Development, 1999. ISBN 156286128X.

Provides examples of successful interactive learning exercises used in distance learning.

◀ Mantyla, Karen, ed. **The 2000/2001 ASTD Distance Learning Yearbook**. New York: McGraw-Hill, 2000/2001. OCLC 44880453.

Articles about distance learning, the formation of distance learning proposals, Web training, videoconferencing, and the administration of such programs.

◀ McMahan, Kevin. **Distance Education Desk Guide Online**. August 1999. http://www.bizresources.com/learning/de_deskguide.html (26 July 2001).

This online document provides excellent information for the online educator. It describes distance learning trends, teaching suggestions, and a list of distance learning programs meant for educators. It also provides a list of resources.

◀ **1999 Distance Education Handbook**. http://www.accjc.org/dislearn .htm (12 August 2001).

This online handbook is a good resource for academic institutions as they plan distance learning programs. It focuses on concerns related to accreditation, such as motivation (an institution's motive for distance education), partnerships and preserving institutional integrity, the institution's mission, educational programs, and the curriculum; faculty, students, library, and learning resources; institutional effectiveness and student outcomes; organization, planning, human resources, facilities, and equipment; catalogs and publications; and intellectual property rights. The handbook includes "Standards and Policies of the Accrediting Commission" for community and junior colleges. The standards and policies review the various facets of institutional operations and outline specific criteria for institutional assessment. Included in the document are: (1) principles of good practice for electronically delivered academic degree and certificate programs; (2) guidelines for distance education (curriculum and instruction), evaluation and assessment, library and learning resources, student resources, facilities, and funding; (3) accreditation standards and standards for educational programs; and (4) a selected bibliography of supporting documents.

◀ Orange, Graham, and Dave Hobbs, eds. **International Perspectives on Tele-Education and Virtual Learning Environments**. Hampshire: Ashgate, 2000. ISBN 0754612023.

Reviews the use of computer network resources in distance education.

◀ **Peterson's Guide to Distance Learning Programs 2001**. Princeton, NJ: Peterson's. ISBN 076890403X.

This guide lists 1,000 degree and certificate programs at nearly 900 accredited institutions that are available electronically for undergraduate and distance learning programs. The indexes provide a listing of individual courses and a geographic breakdown. The guide discloses basic information on each institution, such as course delivery site (e.g., home); media—the way the course is delivered (e.g., via television, videotapes, videoconferencing, interactive television, computer conferencing, e-mail); and services, costs, registration, and contact person. Peterson's also provides sections on student profiles, financial aid, programs, services, tuition, and fees.

◀ Picciano, Anthony G. **Distance Learning: Making Connections Across Virtual Space and Time**. Paramus, NJ: Prentice Hall, 2000. ISBN 0130809004.

This book reviews educational technology in distance education.

◀ Preece, Jenny. **Online Communities: Designing Usability and Supporting Sociability**. New York: John Wiley, 2000. ISBN 0471805998.

Preece reviews the research on the use of virtual space and electronic communication on the Web from a sociological point of view. She focuses on techniques to design and build asynchronous environments that engage and support online communities. Her book is a valuable resource for researchers, developers, and even students who are developing their own online communities.

◀ Richardson, John. **Researching Student Learning: Approaches to Studying in Campus-Based and Distance Education**. Philadelphia: Society for Research into Higher Education and Open University Press, 2000. ISBN 0335205151.

This resource looks at student learning and study skills helpful to students in online environments.

◀ Stevenson, Nancy. **Distance Learning for Dummies**. Indianapolis: IDG Books Worldwide, 2000. ISBN 076450763X.

A book for adults describing distance learning and education through the Internet.

◀ **Teaching and Learning**. Washington, D.C.: Instructional Telecommunications Council, 2000. OCLC 44466348.

Reviews case studies for distance education, telecommunications in higher education, and community colleges in the United States. The book includes an appendix, "Quality Assurance Criteria and Standards for Distance Education."

◀ Tulloch, Jacquelyn B., and John Sneed. **The Survey of Distance Learning Programs in Higher Education**. New York: Primary Research Group, 1999. ISBN 1574400223.

This book reviews distance education and telecommunications at colleges and universities.

◀ White, Ken W., and Bob H. Weight. **The Online Teaching Guide: A Handbook of Attitudes, Strategies, and Techniques for the Virtual Classroom**. Boston: Allyn and Bacon, 2000. ISBN 0205295312.

Through a number of essays, educators reflect on teaching methods, curriculum development, and the use of the Internet and technology in online teaching for higher education. Some of the topics covered are communicating online, a student's perspective of learning online, the syllabus, online facilitation of individual and group discussions, developing effective online organization, and reshaping teaching and learning.

◀ Williams, Marcia L., Kenneth Paprock, and Barbara Covington. **Distance Learning: The Essential Guide**. Thousand Oaks, CA: Sage, 1999. ISBN 0761914412.

Based on a set of "How do I" questions, this book provides the foundation necessary for a quick start to distance teaching. The book is a combination of case studies, tear-out worksheets, and checklists. The authors discuss the tools necessary to adapt to a changing environment along with instructional design strategies for instructors. A practical resource for someone new to distance learning and teaching.

Index